Adams Media
An Imprint of Simon & Schuster, Inc.
57 Littlefield Street
Avon, Massachusetts 02322

For information about special discounts for bulk purchases, please contact Simon & Schuster Special Sales at 1-866-506-1949 or business@simonandschuster.com.

The Simon & Schuster Speakers Bureau can bring authors to your live event. For more information or to book an event contact the Simon & Schuster Speakers Bureau at 1-866-248-3049 or visit our website at www.simonspeakers.com.

Interior photographs: page 15 © Oleksandr Tkachenko/123RF; page 20 © Valery Shanin/123RF; page 32 © Boris Breytman/123RF; page 38 © scusi/123RF; page 47 © Luciano Mortula/123RF; page 52 © Helmut Knab/123RF; page 55 © Clipart.com; page 62 © Ahmet Insan Ariturk/123RF; page 78 © satori/123RF; page 95 © Scott Prokop/123RF; page 103 © godrick/123RF; page 153 from Library of Congress via Wikimedia Commons; page 176 © iStockphoto.com/Ivan Bastien; page 181 © iStockphoto.com/Lingbeek; page 185 by Daniel Case via Wikimedia Commons; page 200 © iStockphoto.com/mjbs; page 230 © sborisov/123RF; page 245 © Alberto Giacomazzi/123RF.

Manufactured in the United States of America

10 9 8 7 6 5 4

Library of Congress Cataloging-in-Publication Data has been applied for.

ISBN 978-1-4405-9007-8
ISBN 978-1-4405-9008-5 (ebook)

ARCHITECTURE 10

FROM **FRANK GEHRY** TO **ZIGGURATS**
—— AN ESSENTIAL GUIDE TO ——
BUILDING STYLES AND **MATERIAL**

NICOLE BRIDGE

Adams Media
New York   London   Toronto   Sydney   New Delhi

DEDICATION

To Cliff, M, C, and J—with love.

ACKNOWLEDGMENTS

I am grateful to all the editors associated with Adams Media who have supported the development of *Architecture 101*, especially Peter Archer for his shrewd editing skills and endless patience.

CONTENTS

INTRODUCTION

In its most basic definition, architecture is the tangible output of planning, design, engineering, and construction. It is the way we have shaped our environment for thousands of years, the process of building the places in which we live our lives. Architecture emerged as humans transitioned from hunter-gatherers to members of settled civilizations. In early Mesopotamia, residential quarters, courtyards, temples, and administrative buildings formed some of the earliest permanent human spaces. These places made it possible to establish agriculture, religious rituals, a government system, and commerce. They were, in short, the first urban communities.

Today, planning and building is still at the center of our society, but we have also come to appreciate the aesthetics of our constructions. We critique their artistic attributes and admire their innovations as if they were on display in a gallery. In this way, architecture has become a massive public art offering. The tension between the need to build structures that are sturdy and safe and the desire to design something that delights us visually is at the crux of architecture's power as an art form. Think of the Empire State Building (1931). The 102 stories on a two-acre plot in the middle of Manhattan constitute an efficient business center, pulsing with more than 150 tenants and seventy-three elevators racing countless employees to their jobs. But when we pass it on the street or see it in the backdrop of a movie or photograph, that limestone and granite façade, the shiny aluminum, the magnificent rows of lights above the observation deck . . . it becomes something more than its function. It is one of the most iconic pieces of Art Deco, a world-recognized emblem of New York City. It is a testament to the power of architecture.

Even those simple houses back in Mesopotamia were beautifully designed. The Sumerians, their builders, took tremendous care to mold clay with their hands into uniform bricks, patiently dry them in the sun, and place them in elegant stacks. Imagine how mesmerizing those intricate, sand-colored cities must have looked against a clear blue sky 5,000 years ago. In good design, form and function have always lived together.

Today's cities are crammed with layers of different styles and designs. Our structures are a way for us to see who we were and admire who we are becoming. One can marvel over the ornate gothic towers such as Beauvais Cathedral (1225) in France and then turn to the Guggenheim Museum Bilbao (1997) in Spain. A triumph in modern architecture, the intertwined glass, titanium, and limestone museum is unapologetically nestled right into the heart of the old Basque city and has become the most recognized structure on its cherished river view.

As Frank Lloyd Wright said, "The mother of art is architecture. Without an architecture of our own we have no soul of our own civilization."

To study architecture is to investigate the heart of our existence. In this space we will examine the great architects, influential styles, and powerful contexts for the most admired and studied structures in the world. Let's take up residence here. Welcome to *Architecture 101*.

THE STONE AGE

The Earliest Human Settlements

In the beginning, humans were entirely preoccupied with the need to find food. Hunting animals and gathering fruit and grains was their means of survival. Their settlements were semi-permanent homes, functioning almost like a base camp, from which the tribes set forth to hunt and forage. Archaeologists have found evidence of huts built on the Central Russian Plain. These human shelters were organized into settlements, some dating as far back as 14,000 B.C.E. Among the creatures these humans hunted were mammoths, ten-foot-tall hairy elephants. They hunted the mammoths for food, but they also used their carcasses for other things like starting fires, manufacturing tools, and constructing huts. The hunters fashioned the bones into a dome, then filled any gaps between the bones with moss and shrubs before covering the whole structure with turf or a mammoth hide. This enterprise required a tremendous amount of resources; depending on the size of the hut, it could take as many as ninety-five mammoths to build a single structure. In fact, scientists are still not sure if the mammoths became extinct because of climate change or whether overhunting had something to do with it. The largest huts were elaborate enough to include multiple hearths on the inside and openings in the top from which smoke could escape.

Features of the Earliest Huts

- Mammoth bones
- Pine poles
- Animal skin linings
- Central hearth

Jericho

Urban civilizations began appearing much later, around 8000 B.C.E., when crop cultivation had begun to produce enough food that people did not have to move around so much. Now not everyone concerned themselves with food collection and production. People separated into other specialties such as warriors and priests. Humans began settling into permanent spaces and these early farming communities grew into villages often five or ten times bigger than the nomadic hunting settlements before them. Jericho was one of these communities.

Jericho was a fortified settlement positioned on the West Bank. Originally built in 8000–7000 B.C.E., it was enclosed and protected by a thick stone wall, in places as high as twelve feet, as well as a ditch. A tower about thirty feet rose over the area. The entire city stretched across some ten acres.

The Power of Mud

The earliest dwellings in Jericho, inhabited by hunters and farmers, were mud huts. Mud brick was the preferred building material in this area for thousands of years. It was easy to work with and manufactured from materials that were cheap and widely available. Builders mixed mud and water together with a binder such as reeds or straw and molded them into rectangles. They then set the bricks out in the sun to bake until they were dry. After the bricks were stacked into the desired shape, the walls of the mud brick houses were plastered and painted.

Honoring the Dead

The early civilizations thought constantly about their ancestors. Even the way they built their homes emphasized this part of their culture. They often buried their dead family members beneath the floors of their homes. In the days immediately following the death, they would decorate makeshift shrines to the deceased in their homes with vibrant wall paintings or carvings. The subject of these paintings, like prehistoric cave paintings, was often hunting scenes, wild animal motifs, and cattle. To create these paintings, they would cover the wall with white plaster, almost like a blank canvas. Then they would use pigments bound with fats to make colorful paints. After the grieving period ended, the family would paint over these shrines. In some areas the skeletons of the dead were decorated. Sometimes the bodies were covered with red ocher or the necks and heads were painted with blue and green pigments. They were often buried with jewelry and weapons.

Jericho Skulls

One of the fascinating artifacts archaeologists uncovered from the ancient site at Jericho were skull "portraits." These were sculptural renderings of a dead person's likeness that were placed over his detached skull. These plastered skulls underscore just how important the dead were to the people of Jericho. They were an art form dedicated to preserving the memory of one who had passed on.

Çatal Hüyük

Çatal Hüyük (c. 6500–5700 B.C.E.) was situated in Anatolia, part of present-day Turkey. It was a highly sophisticated prehistoric city that sat fifty-seven feet above the plain and stretched out over thirty-two acres. Archaeologists have uncovered more than a dozen levels to this settlement, which indicates that it was likely inhabited for thousands of years. They also found evidence of a well-established trading network, agricultural system, and stoneware and ceramics production. More than 1,000 houses made of mud brick and wood were constructed here. There were no streets or outer stone wall like the one built around Jericho. Instead, the houses were densely packed and nestled right next to each other, leaving no gaps. This side-by-side layout of houses formed the perimeter defense wall.

The walls of these houses were made of mud bricks and, since they rested right against each other and the sides were not reachable, each house could only be accessed by the roof. The roofs were held up with heavy wood timbers. These in turn supported smaller timbers covered by reeds and mud. There were also high, small openings in the walls for ventilation. Residents would climb over the rooftops and enter their house by a ladder that went through an opening in the roof. Each house included a main room with raised areas for sitting, preparing food, and sleeping. Many houses also included an oven or hearth, possibly one in the middle of each room, for baking bread and making pottery. A ventilation shaft situated in the ceiling allowed smoke from the ovens and hearths to escape. These homes were built with post-and-lintel construction.

The houses were built over the ruins of older houses. Newer buildings were supported by the ones that came before them, raising the houses to different levels. This practice also created open spaces between houses, where citizens could burn their garbage. Interior room walls were lined with white plaster, and the beams that were used to hold up the roofs were painted red.

Within these tight rows of houses were also shrines dedicated to the inhabitants' deities. These appeared sporadically in the layout, usually windowless and without ornamentation. They sometimes included statues and a simple decorative motif of bulls, symbols of one of the important gods worshipped in the city.

Post and Lintel Construction

This common building technology is found all over the ancient world. Vertical supports (posts) were set in the ground and a horizontal structure (lintel) was balanced on top. The posts support the lintel and its loads without crushing or buckling. This method would later be central to ancient Greek architecture and is still used today for doorways set within walls.

Eventually cities such as Çatal Hüyük were abandoned, possibly because they did not have room for the addition of public buildings. Once people began to establish governments and undertake civic initiatives, they would require more space and deliberate city planning.

MEGALITHIC CONSTRUCTION

The First Stone Builders

In these early days of human civilization, while urban communities were not as widespread in western Europe as they were in Mesopotamia, in the former you could find many megalith constructions. The purpose of these large stone structures still mystifies but archaeologists have formulated some ideas about their uses: possibly they were erected for astronomical observations or to serve as communal tombs for the upper classes. They were likely also used to claim land. More than 500 of these sites have been documented in Ireland alone. There were three different types of these massive stone structures: menhir, dolmen, and cromlech.

Carnac, Brittany, France (c. 4000 B.C.E.)

Carnac, in Brittany, France, contains one of the most extensive menhir assemblies in the world—more than 10,000. The word *menhir* derives from two Celtic words: *men*, meaning "stone," and *hir*, meaning "long." These stones were slightly shaped and placed standing upright into the ground. They often stood individually, but at Carnac they appear in rows. Some people believe that these shapes were phallic and their position is supposed to represent the male fertilizing the earth. Others think the menhirs functioned as a point on a landscape map, suggesting that the area might have been used as an observatory to track the movement of heavenly bodies.

Stonehenge (c. 3100 –c. 1500 B.C.E.)

Henges were made of wood or stone circles. Stonehenge, the most famous of these constructions, is a cromlech. The word *cromlech* derives from the Welsh words *crom*, meaning "curved" or "bent," and *lech* meaning "stone." It is clear that cromlechs were used to mark sacred spaces but their exact purpose is still unknown.

Stonehenge, in particular, began as a ditch running in a circle. Fifty-six pits inside the circular ditch have been excavated; they were filled with rubble or cremated human bones.

Later, sarsen stones (sandstone blocks) were erected in a layout that aligned with midsummer sunrise and midwinter sunset and the positions of the moon. The stones stand on a slightly sloping ridge with a mile-long road that runs east to west. In form Stonehenge consists of a series of concentric circles and U shapes. The outer circle is a post-and-lintel construction with blocks of stone thirteen feet high. The blocks are rough on the outside and a little bit smoother on the inside, and each stone tapers slightly at the top.

To secure the outer circle at Stonehenge, a tenon projects from each post. This tenon then fits into a hole that has been carved into the lintil. For the outer wall of structures, the lintels were slightly curved, creating a circle when they are all attached end to end. The inner circle is formed from single upright bluestones. These include five large trilithons that are arranged in a U shape. Then there is an even smaller U shape of bluestones that echoes the shape of the five posts-and-lintels. Within this U, one lone stone lies on the ground. This has been called the Altar Stone, although its true use is not certain.

Many of the original stones at Stonehenge have now fallen but those that are still standing show us a shadow of how impressive must have been the original monument. They have become one of the biggest tourist attractions in Britain.

Eventually a new group of settlers brought their pottery skills and new building techniques into the area. These settlers, called the Beaker People, are believed to have completed Stonehenge. Somehow, they managed to bring in huge sandstone blocks from a village that was about twenty miles away. No one knows for certain how the community managed to achieve this incredible feat.

Dolmens

Dolmens (the word comes from the Celtic word *dol* which means "table") are large, flat stones that are supported by two or more upright stones; think of it as the construction of a table. Dolmens could be constructed to form single-chamber tombs. These were usually covered with earth or smaller stones to form a burial mound. Later, additions were made to the dolmens that turned them into passageways. Dolmens may have also been used to mark the boundaries of settlement territories. Sometimes the walls inside a dolmen were decorated with carvings or paintings.

Mysteries of the Stones

Archaeologists do not know how the massive stones that make up Stonehenge were brought to the site. The bluestones weigh as much as four tons each and the largest sandstones weigh as much as fifty tons. No one has any idea how the lintels were placed either. Scientists are constantly uncovering more information about the megaliths but we still do not know for certain for what purpose these structures were used. It is clear that there is some common purpose, since henges appear throughout Europe. The people who lived during these times were tremendously impacted by seasonal changes. Some archaeologists think these henges were the sites of dances, spring and summer celebrations, and processions dedicated to the change in season.

Another possibility stems from the construction of the megaliths at Stonehenge. These structures do not include roofs. Perhaps they were used as astronomical observatories to help keep track of time and the motion of the stars, including the sun. These monuments were situated according to positions of the sun and the moon at particular times of the year. Even the road is aligned with the rising summer sun.

As the use of metal increased starting around 2000 B.C.E., the prevalence of these massive stone monuments began to decline.

MESOPOTAMIA

Developing the Fertile Crescent

The earliest literate civilizations lived in the area between the Tigris and Euphrates Rivers (modern-day Iraq). This area, which historians refer to as the Fertile Crescent, was called Mesopotamia from the Greek meaning "the land between two rivers." The fertile plains in this region are where writing began and the first major urban centers were organized.

The City of Ur

Ur was situated in what is now southern Iraq. It was a powerful, wealthy city. In fact, much of what we know about ancient history in general begins at Ur because it is here that archaeologists have found large collections of clay tablets. In the early Bronze Age (c. 3300–2000 B.C.E.) people started to write things down, record history, and keep track of laws. The ziggurat in this city was surrounded by other public buildings, with all enclosed by a double wall. A big mausoleum called the Royal Cemetery of Ur was located just outside of the wall. The contents of this cemetery later gave archaeologists a clue about just how prosperous Ur had been; here they found the remains of chariots, harps, and jewelry. They also found the bodies of people who may have been killed so that they could be buried with the dead as companions. Main residences were located beyond this enclosed area. Ur's harbors saw a lively shipping trade on the Euphrates.

This area of the plains was prone to flooding, so the entire city was raised on a high earthen mound. A giant fortified wall further protected the entire city.

The houses were situated in densely packed neighborhoods with open courtyards and windows facing these so that fresh air could enter the rooms. The side of the house that faced the street featured a plain brick wall. This continues to be a common urban layout in Mediterranean and Middle Eastern communities today.

Characteristics of Architecture in Mesopotamia
- Mud bricks
- Tripartite design, meaning plans organized around three rooms
- Courtyards
- Reed roofs

The Ziggurat of Ur

Ziggurats were seen by their builders as a link between heaven and earth. These temples were built by Sumerian farmers who worked on them between planting and harvest seasons. It took millions of mud bricks to form these enormous structures. The builders formed the bricks into a large rectangle with inward sloping walls and a series of platform steps. Sun-dried mud bricks were very strong but they were also porous, which meant that they would not hold together very well in the rain. To add waterproofing to the ziggurats, the builders created another set of bricks that would be more resilient in bad weather. This second set was fired in a kiln and then stacked in front of the mud bricks as a protective shell. These buildings were placed on raised ground to provide protection from the floodwaters that were such an integral part of life in this region.

The shape of the ziggurats evolved over time. In the beginning the temple was set on a platform on top of the pyramid. Then additional platforms were added on top of these first platforms. These layers formed stepped towers. This design was intended to elevate the tower to the gods so that they could descend from the heavens to bring prosperity to the community. The ziggurat's shape was reminiscent of the mountains from which the Sumerians had migrated, which they thought would make the gods feel at home in their new territory.

The Ziggurat of Ur was dedicated to Nanna, the moon god, around 2100 B.C.E. It was so large that it could be seen for miles across the plains. A shrine was situated at the top, accessible only to the most important people in the city. The shrine has since disappeared, so little is known about it. Aside from that, the ziggurat of Ur is one of the best preserved structures from ancient Mesopotamia. There were other temples at Ur but this was considered to be the most important because it was dedicated to the protective god of Ur.

Protecting Ancient Architecture

Time is unkind to architecture. Human traffic and weather wear on ancient sites. Builders can be unsentimental when planning for new developments, and raze existing structures. The ravages of war are of concern for many sites in today's Middle East. Archaeologists and preservationists find themselves arguing to protect ancient sites in areas where the circumstances of human life and death are so devastating that it is difficult to ask communities to think about anything else. The World Monuments Fund is an advocacy group that raises money and awareness and partners with the people living in these areas, like government and museum officials, to save these sites from destruction. The Ziggurat of Ur and the city of Babylon are among the many sites in this area included on the Fund's watch list.

BABYLON
An Architecture-Minded King

After the last Sumerian king was overthrown by foreign invaders, Mesopotamia was divided into independent city-states. Among them was a group of people from Arabia who established Babylon as their capital. Babylon is considered by many to be the greatest of all the ancient Mesopotamian cities, in part because it was the first product of thoughtful, deliberate city planning. Constructed more than 2,600 years ago in biblical times, the gorgeous city, in what is now Iraq, straddled the two banks of the Euphrates River and was protected by a wall that circled the entire perimeter.

Important Rulers of Babylon
- King Hammurabi (died 1750 B.C.E.)
- Cyrus the Great (c. 576–530 B.C.E.)
- Nebuchadnezzar II (c. 634–562 B.C.E.)
- Alexander the Great (356–323 B.C.E.)

Nebuchadnezzar II

For two and a half centuries, Babylon was ruled by Assyria until a new southern dynasty managed to regain power. Nebuchadnezzar, the strongest neo-Babylonian king, put much effort into restoring the former glory of Babylon. He was also responsible for the best architecture in the city. His palace and the Tower of Babel, two of the best-known structures from this period, were made of mud bricks. The Tower of Babel refers to the ziggurat, which was dedicated to the god Marduk.

Ishtar Gate

Another fruit of Nebuchadnezzar's initiative was the Ishtar Gate. The thirty-eight-foot-tall gate was placed at the main entrance to the city and dedicated to the goddess Ishtar, who was the reigning goddess of fertility, love, war, and sex. Some of the blue-glazed bricks bore yellow and white motifs of animals such as lions, bulls, dragons, and aurochs (an extinct type of wild cattle) to show honor to other deities including Adad, the god of weather, and Marduk, the chief god of Babylon.

Glazing

Glazing is a technique for waterproofing clay objects. Usually the glaze was made with ground mineral pigments mixed with water, at which point color could also be added. The effect is a glass-like finish that, when fired together, adheres to the clay bricks.

The gate was crenelated at the top, and if you look closely you can see that the crenels are little ziggurats. Directly behind the gate was a brick road called Processional Way, which was a half mile long with high walls.

An arch, such as the Ishtar Gate, is stronger than a simple post-and-lintel construction and represents a considerable advance in building technique. The reason is that the round arch carries the weight onto two vertical supports. On the lintel, all the stress rests on the horizontal. The arch effectively functions as a curved lintel, connected to the two posts on either side.

The Original Ishtar Gate

Many years ago European archaeologists packed up many of the mud bricks and artifacts and brought them back to their home countries. Among the relics they took was the original Ishtar Gate, which was sent to Germany. It is now on exhibit at the Berlin Museum of the Ancient Near East (the Pergamonmuseum).

The Hanging Gardens of Babylon

The Hanging Gardens of Babylon, long considered one of the Seven Wonders of the World, were another part of Nebuchadnezzar II's plan to make Babylon beautiful beyond all other cities. These were a series of roof terraces that had manmade irrigation. The gardens could be accessed through the palace. Mesopotamia was extremely dry so it would have been a major undertaking to keep the gardens watered and healthy. Water would have needed to be brought in from the Euphrates constantly. Some historians believe the irrigation system involved a slave-operated machine that stretched from the gardens to the river, dunking buckets into the water and carrying them up to a reservoir in the garden terraces. Imagine how beautiful and exotic these lush green gardens must have looked in this clay-colored city.

Hanging Gardens of Babylon . . . not in Babylon?

A recent study out of Oxford University challenges the history and location of the Hanging Gardens of Babylon. One academic spent nearly two decades studying cuneiform tablets and searching for evidence of the irrigation systems to learn more about the gardens' mysterious history. Painstaking research and excavations revealed evidence of incredible canals and aqueducts in what is today Northern Iraq. This could mean that King Sennacherib of Assyria may have actually built the gardens in Nineveh!

Taking Care of the Ruins

In recent years there has been a lot of squabbling over the ruins at Babylon. Saddam Hussein tried to rebuild them in the 1980s but he used cheap modern materials for the foundation, which some scientists believe actually did more damage to the ruins. He also included motifs of himself around the resurrected monuments. The war in Iraq may have caused further damage, especially when the Americans built a military base in that region. Some in Iraq have lobbied for excavating the city once more but many are afraid that it would be far more damaging to expose such an archaeological marvel in a country that is experiencing great political instability and social unrest.

The city began to decline around 538 B.C.E. when it was conquered by Cyrus the Great and the Persians. Generally, the ruins in Mesopotamia have not lasted as well as the ruins in, say, Greece, because mud bricks are not a long-term building material.

ANCIENT EGYPT

A Triumph in Geometry

The civilization of Egypt grew to power on the Nile River, a location that influenced everything about its life. The river flows north from central Africa to the Mediterranean Sea. Each year, usually sometime in August, the rains in central Africa and melting snows in the Ethiopian highlands cause the river to flood to a level of nearly twenty-five feet. The flooding was enough to put the entire Nile Valley under water. When the waters finally receded, they left a dark, rich silt that was perfect for growing crops. Although the annual flood sounds destructive, it restored fertility to the land and led to a new farming season. Egypt has been called the gift of the Nile. The villages were far back enough from the plain that they were spared and the water always stopped right at the desert. When the waters had receded, the farmers would begin a new planting campaign.

On the strength of this pattern, civilization along the Nile grew to immense size and power. The state was ruled by a pharaoh, whose descendants formed his dynasty. The early dynastic period of ancient Egypt began around 3100 B.C.E.

The Egyptians, both highborn and low, lived their lives to the rhythm of the Nile's flood. They kept track of the moon and sun phases so they could predict the timing of the waters. This constant monitoring of nature's patterns gave form to their religion. They subscribed to polytheism (belief in many gods) and attributed all things in nature to those gods. They welcomed the gods of other faiths and integrated them into their own theology.

Egyptians also put a lot of stock in the afterlife. They dedicated tremendous time and resources to what they believed to be the critical transition from living to death. To them, death was not the end of life; it was the movement to a different life, on another plain, that was similar to the one just lived. To usher people into their new lives, the Egyptians often preserved the dead with the utmost thoughtfulness and elegant ritual. They mummified the bodies and buried them with their favorite earthly possessions. They did it in a big way—and then they did it in a humongous way.

Pyramids

Mastabas were single-story trapezoidal structures, precursors to the pyramids. In the mastaba, the body was placed in a sarcophagus and then buried underground in a single chamber. In another room at the ground level the statue of the deceased was placed. A third room was for receiving mourners who would come bearing gifts and offerings. Families would add chambers in which to bury additional family members.

In about 2700 B.C.E., the Egyptians began to build pyramids and continued to do so for the next thousand years. The first stage in this was the genesis of step pyramids. These were formed by placing mastabas on top of mastabas. There might be as many as five, each structure a little bit smaller than the one beneath it.

Where the Egyptians really outdid themselves was with the geometric pyramids, the most famous of which were built in Giza around 2500 B.C.E. The pyramids at Giza were massive and even today they remain the largest structures built from stone anywhere. Each was positioned on the west bank of the Nile facing the direction of the sunset, a position that symbolized death. They were named for three pharaohs: Khufu, Khafre, and Menkaure. Each pyramid was connected by an elevated road to its own temple where ceremonies were performed and funerary offerings were made. We know little of how they were constructed; one estimate is that groups of 100,000 men must have labored for three months at a time on the project.

The Pyramid of Khufu

The Great Pyramid, Pyramid of Khufu, is the largest of the three and covers thirteen square acres. The base makes a perfect square. Even though it stretches out over so much land, the ground was leveled so precisely that there is only a one-inch margin of difference anywhere at the entire base of the structure. The four sides are exactly even in size. What is even more incredible is that the relation of the length of each side to its height is the same as the relation to a circle's circumference to its radius (better known as pi). Since pi had not been discovered at the time of the Great Pyramid's construction, this relationship is likely just a coincidence. In any case, the pyramids were a triumph of architecture and geometry that continue to amaze.

In its interior, the Great Pyramid includes several rooms for housing the pharaoh's body and the possessions he loved most in his life. Builders used local limestone for the core of the structure and red granite to construct the rooms inside it. The burial chamber was usually placed either underneath the pyramid or in the middle. Khufu's tomb, in particular, was buried slightly less than halfway between the ground and the top of the pyramid in a chamber that is thirty-four feet by seventeen feet. His sarcophagus was so big that the tomb had to be built around it; it would never have fit through a door. The burial chamber is accessible by a sloping walkway. Above this room is a huge gallery with a corbeled roof.

Wear and Tear

The pyramids, although still standing today, have faced intense wear and tear over their four-thousand-year lifespan. Even though the burial chambers and tombs were sealed, grave robbers still managed to get in and steal most of the artifacts. When a terrible earthquake in 1222 damaged many of the buildings in Cairo, the people took stones from the pyramids to patch holes in those structures. This looting actually reduced the height of the Great Pyramid by about twenty-five feet.

The Sphinx

This statue of an enormous human head situated on top of a lion's body crouches near the pyramids of Giza. The statue possibly represents the pharaoh Khafre (also spelled Khafra). The sphinx's head is surrounded by a head cloth, similar to pharaohs' traditional costume, and it faces the sun, suggesting an identification with the sun god Ra, also characteristic of Egyptian royalty.

Pyramid Tours

When you look at pictures of the pyramids they appear to be spread out over an immense desert landscape. They are really only about thirty minutes from downtown Cairo; the area is accessible by bus or metro. Tours are available every day of the week. To view them you must purchase an entrance ticket, which operates as a pass to see several tombs and pyramids. Visitors can also view royal tombs and ancient roadways. These tours are particularly powerful at sunrise and sunset because of the play of the light on the structures.

Temples

In the later centuries of their civilization, Egyptians built a number of elaborate temples where people could come and worship the gods. People were not really supposed to enter the temples but instead stand near them and watch processions of priests and royalty from the outside walls. Since only the priests and pharaohs went inside, their interiors and what went on in them were shrouded with mystery.

The structures were often constructed using the post-and-lintel system. The columns were carved to resemble organic forms such as bundles of papyrus reeds. These temples were called pylons because of the two big sloping walls (pylons) that formed the entrance. The entrances were usually further emphasized with large statues or obelisks on either side. Obelisks are tall four-sided pillars with a pointed tip that resemble tall monuments with a pyramid on top. Often, in ancient times, they were carved from a single stone. Through the entrance to the temple was a large courtyard and then hall with massive columns that were shadowed by clerestory windows that let in small amounts of light.

A Modern Obelisk

The Washington Monument in Washington, D.C., sometimes affectionately referred to as the Big Pencil because of its shape, is an obelisk made of marble, granite, and stone. It is the world's tallest obelisk at more than 554 feet. The monument was built in honor of George Washington shortly after his death. In another nod to Egyptian architecture, the front entrance used to include a carved winged sun, which was later removed from the monument.

MYCENAEAN CIVILIZATION

Cyclopean Construction

Mycenaean civilization, a precursor to classical Greek civilization, flourished between 1600 and 1100 B.C.E. during the Bronze Age. The Mycenaean people were warlike folk who inhabited a rocky hill above the Argive plain on mainland Greece, from which they controlled the main road between Corinth and Argos. As a defensive measure, the city was built on high ground in between mountains. Eventually, the Mycenaeans added walls to provide additional fortification to the city-state.

The Mycenaean walls were enormous, up to twenty-four feet thick and forty feet high in some places. They were so big that when the Greeks happened upon them later, they believed that they had been built by giants or Cyclopes. Their confusion inspired the word *cyclopean* to describe construction with massive stones. Some of the stones used to build these walls weighed as much as ten tons.

The stones were of different shapes but were laid very close together without using any mortar. Sometimes the Mycenaeans used earth and rubble to fill in gaps at the outer layers of the walls, especially in areas where the walls were thicker. To enter Mycenae, one would have to follow a narrow passageway that ran parallel to one of their large defense walls. This, in itself, was a defensive structure since it allowed the Mycenaeans time to attack any intruders before they even reached the front gate.

Lion Gate

There were a number of gates and entrances into the Mycenaean settlement but the front gate, called Lion Gate, was the most imposing. A product of post-and-lintel construction, it was built with upright, very plain stones with a 14-ton lintel lying across the top of them. The top of the gate was a corbeled arch, consisting of stones laid on top of each other progressively until they met at the top to form an arch. At the top point of the arch was a triangular stone that was carved with a relief of lions facing a column, their feet perched on an altar. This triangle is called a relieving triangle because it lessoned the weight on the lintel. The column on the Lion Gate is a symbol of the nature goddess of whom the lions acted as guardians. Their heads were carved separately and attached to the gate with stone pegs called dowels. This made them look as if they were protruding from the gate. The heads have long since fallen off the gate but the dowel holes are still visible.

Corbeling

Corbeling was very popular in Mycenaean architecture. This building technique was used to create not only arches (called corbel arches) but also roofs for circular tombs (called corbel vaults). Corbeled constructions generally made use of a triangular relieving stone.

Megaron

Most Mycenaean cities centered on a large palace complex called a megaron, which translates as "large room." The megaron plan was a rectangular shape with a three-part sequence: porch, vestibule, and a domos. This layout was the precursor to the ancient Greek temples that would become some of the most inspiring architectural structures in the history of the world.

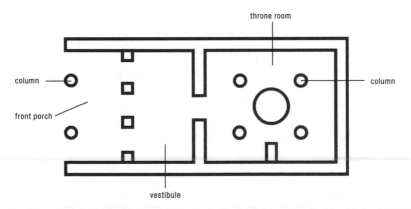

A person entered the megaron through an open porch supported by two columns. The depth of these entrances was longer than the width, an aesthetic point that would become a distinguishing feature of the megaron. Next the visitor passed through an antechamber before entering the throne room. A circular hearth surrounded by four columns was positioned at the center of the throne room, and the king's throne faced the hearth. Above the hearth a hole, called an oculus, punctured the ceiling and allowed for ventilation. The room would have been colorful and topped with a tile roof. Lavishly decorated shrines that displayed precious objects and painted pottery were built within the palaces.

The roofs and upper stories of the palace were framed in wood. It is hard to know exactly what the roofs looked like because they did not survive the test of time, but they were probably flat. (The only reason we can see the foundations today is because they were constructed with stone.) The floors were made of clay, and outdoor courtyards were paved in stone.

Additional Features of the Megaron

- Four wooden columns supported the ceiling
- A second, smaller hall, called the queen's megaron
- Private apartments and areas for administration, storage, and manufacturing
- Painted plaster floors
- Fresco paintings
- Columns and ceilings made of painted wood but sometimes including bronze details
- Rubble-filled crossbeam walls
- Limestone blocks on the exterior walls

Treasury of Atreus

The largest structure at Mycenae was the Treasury of Atreus (sometimes also referred to as the Tomb of Agamemnon, who was Atreus's son). This enormous structure was a tholos, meaning "round building." A visitor entered the tholos through a *dromos*, which is a roadway that serves as an entrance to a building. This roadway, made with rectangular stone blocks, was 118 feet long. The entrance to the tholos was a rectangular doorway. Above it was an enormous lintel that weighed about 100 tons. A relieving triangle was positioned above the lintel, similar to the one that appeared on the Lion Gate. This triangle relieved the lintel from the weight of the ceiling, instead sending the weight to the walls, which prevented the structure from crumbling.

The tholos also served as a tomb. Some people call the tholos a beehive tomb because of its shape. After a dead body had been placed inside, the door was secured with stones. If another body needed to be buried, it could be reopened. These tombs were built into the earth and were accessible through an entrance that may have been elaborately decorated, possibly with bronze plates. However, there is no way to prove this since all the tholoi we know of were plundered long ago. The only thing visible when the tholos was closed was the mound that covered the tomb and the dromos. The weight of the earthen mound over the tholos actually makes the structure more stable.

The decline of Mycenaean civilization began 1200–1100 B.C.E. Some historians believe it was due to a wave of nomadic invaders who used more advanced weaponry. The Mycenaeans had bronze weapons, which could not compete with iron alternatives. A dark age followed in which invading tribes took over the area. Eventually, classical Greece arose on the ruins of this difficult time.

CLASSICAL GREECE

Rising out of the Dark Age

After the Mycenaean stronghold on the culture of southern Greece receded, the golden age of ancient Greece rose out of the darkness. The population on the Greek peninsula expanded, and people searched for arable land that could be colonized. The result was an explosion of new cities across the Greek peninsula.

The new settlements were usually laid out in a very orderly fashion in long rectangular blocks. At the center of each block was the market, along with public areas for recreation and entertainment. A fortification surrounded the entire colony.

Also in the center of these cities were temples to the gods, along with other important buildings. The Greeks modeled the first temples after the simple homes that people built for everyday living. These temples were the most important architectural creations of the Greek builders who lived during the Archaic period (800–480 B.C.E.).

Temple of Hera at Olympia

The first temples were simple one-room buildings that held a statue of a deity. They included a covered porch, or portico, at the entrance and had mud brick walls and a thatched roof.

Most of these buildings have not survived the ravages of time, but the Temple of Hera at Olympia (c. 600–590 B.C.E.) is one of the earliest temples of the Archaic age that we can still see. The innermost room of the temple, called a cella, was built with limestone and sat behind columns. The upper portion of the temple was sun-dried brick; the rest was wood. The roof was tiled. The original wood columns were later replaced with stone, possibly so that they would be strong enough to hold up the tile roof. Tile represented a considerable improvement over thatched roofs, since it was sturdier and less inclined to catch fire.

The Orders

Columns as they appear in Greek architecture were heavily influenced by Egyptian precedent. The Greeks elaborated on these simple structures to develop a set of rules that were used to design buildings during the Classical period. These principles applied to the column and all its parts and divided column styles into three orders. Using the orders was a way to keep things proportionate and clear. The Temple of Hera was built in the Doric order.

The main orders in Greek building are:

- Ionic columns: These columns are more slender than other varieties and sit on a base of stacked disks. Scrolls usually appear at the top. Shafts can be fluted or plain. Typically used for upper levels.
- Corinthian columns: The top of the column (the capital) is adorned with flowers and leaves and flares outward, which gives a sense of height. The shaft is grooved. Since it was slender, it was typically used for the upper levels.
- Doric columns: Typically used for the lower levels of multistory buildings because they were thicker. Smooth, rounded capitals, unadorned; the shaft is grooved and wider at the bottom.

Even after the Greek builders began using stone for walls and columns, they continued for a long time to use wood frames for the roofs.

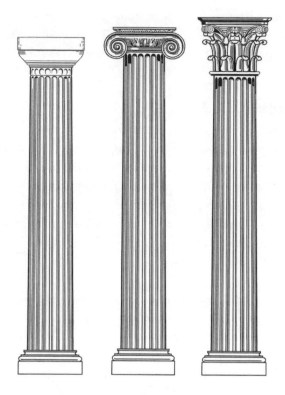

Parts of the Column System

The entablature is the continuous lintel propped up by the columns. The entablature holds the architrave, frieze, and cornice. The architrave is the lowest part of the entablature and the frieze sits just above it and is usually carved or sculpted with decoration. The cornice is the piece of molding just beneath the ceiling. The abacus is the flat, square block that transitions the column to the architrave.

Building Materials

Greek temples were built with local materials such as marble and limestone. Sometimes builders would grind marble down into a stucco that could be applied over limestone as a protective coating. Marble was sturdier and resilient to the elements so it did not require any additional protection. The weight of the materials influenced the size and shape of these buildings. The lintel could not span too great a distance or else it would crack in the middle. The columns also needed to be a certain diameter to support the tile roof. The columns at the Temple of Hera swell at the base and then diminish in size as they get closer to the capital.

Entasis

Change in column diameter is called entasis; it was a way to combat optical illusion. When columns are placed together in a row, they give the impression they are bent. Entasis is a subtle convexity added to columns to make them look straight to the eye.

Flutes are grooves that run down the shaft of the column. Each flute is defined by the raised edges on either side of the groove. This edge is called an arris.

The Parthenon

The Parthenon in Athens was the largest structure built during the Classical period of Greek architecture (510–323 B.C.E.). The Parthenon we see today was actually built to replace one that burned to the ground when the Persians ransacked Athens in 480 B.C.E. The original structure was built from the most superior marble of Mount Pentelicus.

The structure that remains today is a Doric temple eight columns wide and seventeen feet deep. The columns supported a continuous frieze around the exterior of the cella wall. The Delian League Treasury was housed in the back room of the temple. The Delian League was an alliance of the heads of Greek city-states. The League's treasury room was designed with Ionic attributes including four Ionic columns that supported the roof.

The Doric columns at the Parthenon are elongated to a slenderness that is almost Ionic. The end columns are slightly closer together than those in the middle. The slight variations in the way the columns are placed lend liveliness to the building's composition. Slight bulges in the columns make them appear to be very straight. The outer columns also lean inward by six centimeters to combat the optical illusion that would make them appear as if they were falling outward. The spacing and sizing of these columns was an incredible aesthetic innovation.

Although we're used to seeing the temple in stark white, like the bleached bones of an ancient beast, the original temple was painted gold, red, and blue. It must have been stunning against the clear blue Mediterranean sky. The exterior and interior of the Parthenon were filled with sculptures, also painted, depicting the birth of Athena and the contest between Athena and Poseidon to control Athens.

Triglyphs are the periodic tablets with vertical grooves that appear on the Doric frieze. Metopes are the square spaces that appear between the triglyphs. At the Parthenon, the metopes included relief sculptures of struggles between Greeks and Amazons, Trojans, gods and giants. The continuous frieze around the cella wall is inside the colonnade and illustrates a procession of Athenians bringing gifts to Athena at the Panathenaea, a festival in her honor. Much of this powerful frieze was destroyed in 1687 when a Venetian shell hit a Turkish magazine that was stored inside the building.

The Spread of Corinthian Columns

The Corinthian column gained popularity in the fourth century. Such columns were usually incorporated as an additional feature on an otherwise Doric or Ionic building.

The Acropolis

The term *acropolis* refers to any city settlement that is built on a hill or other elevated area. In Athens, the Parthenon sits astride a limestone plateau that is home to a number of other magnificent classical monuments. Its initial function was as a fortified citadel but after a while its purpose became strictly religious. Pericles (c. 495–429 B.C.E.), a powerful Greek statesman, heavily promoted arts and literature, partly inspiring the city's golden age. It was essentially his public works initiative that generated most of the construction on the Acropolis. It provided jobs to the people and began a movement to beautify the city.

THE HELLENISTIC AGE

The Spread of Greek Culture

The golden age of Athens began to fade during the Peloponnesian War, fought for more than twenty-five years between the Athenian empire and the Peloponnesian League, led by Sparta. In the end, Sparta won the war, and Athens was left in ruins. It would never really bounce back. In 338 B.C.E. a new power from the north appeared, when Philip II of Macedon annexed all of Greece. His son, Alexander, took the throne in 336 after Philip's assassination and set his sights on expanding his growing empire. He raced through most of the civilized world, conquering and snatching up land, largely from the Athenians' ancient enemy, the Persians. He went far, crossing the Mediterranean and heading into North Africa and southwest Asia. Finally, at the borders of India, his generals persuaded him to turn back. It was one of the greatest campaigns of conquest in the history of the world.

Wherever he went, Alexander spread Greek culture and integrated it with local customs and arts. For this reason, the period between his death in 323 B.C.E. and the beginning of the Roman Empire (c. 31 B.C.E.) is known as the Hellenistic Age. It marks the transition of Greek society from autonomous city-states to its folding into this larger region. Art and architecture during this period were the result of direct influence of Greek culture across the new empire.

Hellenistic Architecture and Art

Unlike the classical Greek art that came before it, Hellenistic art and literature emphasized the *real* instead of the *ideal*. Popular themes explored daily life in the world of humans, gods, and heroes. The idea was to give viewers an experience of something theatrical. Architecture was freer and more ornate with showy ornamentation. Buildings were bigger and grander. Although the Corinthian order had been developed during the late Classical period, it came into its full glory at this time. The Doric order, characterized by its austerity and discipline, was not as popular for Hellenistic temples. The meticulous coordination of column spacing that was characteristic of the Doric was not necessary for Ionic or Corinthian orders.

During this time, mainland Greece did not have the resources for major building initiatives so most of the existing examples of Hellenistic temples are found on Asia Minor.

The Great Altar of Zeus at Pergamum

Pergamum was the capital city of the Kingdom of Pergamum, which was famous for its monumental collection of architecture on its acropolis. The altar of Zeus, chief of the gods, was a horseshoe-shaped building that was Ionic in its design. It was raised on a platform and fitted with a wide staircase positioned at the entrance. Its large frieze was decorated with relief sculpture that demonstrates the emotional nature of Hellenistic work. Two friezes depicted dramatic retellings of battles between Celtic tribes. Among the images is one of a Gallic chief killing himself and his wife. Another scene shows a battle between Athena and the giant Alkyoneus, with Athena grabbing his hair and pulling his head back. The drilling is deep on these sculptures so the relief appears very high, which means that the shadows and light against it are powerful. It makes the sculpture come to life and brings a humanity and naturalism to the figures represented. At times, they almost seem to hang off the frieze.

The Temple of Apollo Epicurius at Bassae

The Temple of Apollo Epicurius at Bassae (450–425 B.C.E.) was built to honor Apollo Epicurius, a healer who had come to the aid of the people of Philagia when they were beset by plague. This temple was built in a rural setting so far from the city that it was not even discovered until 1765 when a French architect happened upon it. The structure rises over 1,100 feet high in the mountains of the Arcadia region in the heart of Peloponnesus. The temple was built from gray limestone that had been quarried locally.

Alexandria of Egypt

Alexandria of Egypt was founded by Alexander himself (one of a number of cities he founded on his travels) and ruled by the Ptolemies, a dynasty that survived Alexander and continued to be a power in the Mediterranean until the time of the Roman Empire. The city was the center of commerce and culture, the most influential city of the empire. The Tomb of Alexander the Great was here, as well as one of the greatest libraries in the ancient world, sadly destroyed by subsequent generations of raiders and religious mobs.

This structure stands out especially because it involves all three orders. The longer side of the structure holds fifteen columns. At either end of the shorter sides of the rectangle are six columns, combining Ionic and Corinthian orders to make a colonnade that is quiet and serene. This mixing of orders was artistically daring for that time.

Inside the cella are a series of Ionic columns that are imbedded in the walls; this is also notable because Ionic had not traditionally been used for the interior of a cella. The cella itself was a simple, windowless, rectangular room with an entrance located behind the portico façade. One single Corinthian column is situated inside of the cella near the *adyton,* which was a private section of the building not open to the public. Temple leaders were the only people permitted into the adyton. This column holds one of the earliest examples of a Corinthian capital.

There were twenty-two sculpted plates on the Ionic frieze. For decoration, the walls and column bases were made from limestone, while the Ionic capitals and Corinthian capital were made from marble. Metopes of the exterior frieze of the cella were constructed of marble.

City Planning

One of the Greek traditions that spread through the Hellenistic Age was the grid city plan. In this plan, a rectangular grid was set around central public spaces. Slight adjustments could be made for varying terrains. This plan is still popular in today's modern cities such as New York City.

HINDU TEMPLES
Honoring the Gods

Ancient Indian civilization is sometimes known as the Harappan civilization, named for Harappan, one of the cities in the Indus River Valley. Even though ancient India is believed to be the largest of all the early civilizations, evidence of its existence was not found until the early 1920s and so we are still learning a lot about it. The people of the Harappan civilization were involved in trade networks with Mesopotamia and lived in efficiently planned cities with roads and drainage systems. They were mostly agrarian without an oppressive class structure. The main religion was Hinduism, which blended culture and traditions from all over the area.

Angkor Wat

Angkor Wat (early twelfth century C.E.) was a monumental Hindu temple complex built in the great city of Angkor. It was an enormous complex of interconnected waterways, roads, monasteries, and shrines that covers almost one square mile. The city of Angkor was a thirty-one-square-mile city located on the Cambodian plain.

The temple complex was intended to represent Mount Meru. In the Hindu faith, Mount Meru is home to the gods, and the five peaks on the mountain represent the center of the universe. The mountain itself lies at the axis of the Hindu cosmos. The outside walls of the complex were thought of as the mountains that, in the Hindu tradition, mark the edge of the cosmos. Around them was a circle of artificial moats, canals, and reservoirs.

These waterways provided irrigation for the rice paddies that secured agricultural success and prosperity to the city and the temple's inhabitants. The temple itself was dedicated to Vishnu and also used as a tomb for Suryavarman II, its builder. It faces the west, where the dead are believed to depart.

Orientation to the West

The fact that the temple complex is oriented to the west and not the east suggested to some architectural historians the dedication to Vishnu, since Vishnu is more associated with the west. Others concluded that Suryavarman intended from the beginning for the building to serve as his tomb, since souls in the afterlife pass west rather than east.

A stone causeway leads from the moat to the big entrance and then to the enclosure of the temple space. The main roadway is flanked by balustrades that are in the shape of giant water serpents, symbols of cosmic fertility. The main temple building is three stories with corner towers pitched at each tier. These towers have porticos, which create a tiered presentation on a vertical plane. There are then repeating horizontal bands. The entire design is a two- and three-dimensional mandala of the cosmos. There are steep steps leading up to the pavilions and another set of steps leading to the central tower.

The structure is made of sandstone and volcanic rock. Motifs are carved into the materials throughout the complex. The temple includes many courtyards and terraces that in turn contain statues. A striking section of these sculptures is found on the internal walls of the lowest open gallery, which contain over a mile of beautifully carved bas-reliefs that are larger than life. These lively carvings depict Suryavarman II and the deeds of the gods.

A Monument Abandoned

After about 300 years, the city of Angkor was abandoned, and the jungle gradually grew over much of it. The temple was inhabited by Buddhist monks and was a place of pilgrimage to both Hindus and Buddhists for a long time, but many European travelers could not get through the dense jungle to see its glories. The temple complex had something of the complexion of a lost world. In the 1860s, colonial French discovered the site and initiated a program to reconstruct and preserve it.

Features of Hindu Temples

- *Garbha griha*, or "womb chamber," an interior sanctuary that houses an image of the temple's main deity or cult image. It is a small, windowless, square-shaped cella.

- The interior is a dark space illuminated by oil lamps and smelling of incense
- Thick ceiling and cella walls

Significant Sites

Some evidence suggests that the earliest sacred structures on the Indian subcontinent were *vedikas*, stone railings that encircled spiritually significant areas marked by trees and stones. Brahmin priests developed open-air fire altars that were constructed and designed by using a rigid geometric format and system. Hindu temples were built with very sophisticated mathematical systems. The *Shilpa Shastras* texts codify the system that was used to build them. The temples were believed to be a way to anchor a sacred space in the world and channel its divine energy.

Temple Construction

In temple construction, first the builders choose a sacred site. They take several years to purify the ground and rid it of evil spirits. Sacred cows graze the site to enhance the fertility of the land. Next the temple's plan and design is laid out. The proportions are organized around a unit of measure that is calibrated by cosmic harmony. Finally, the foundation stones are set in place.

Most temples were made out of stone, following a post-and-lintel system. Their lintels projected forward from the doorways and were held in place with strong clamps made of iron. Doors were made of wood.

ANCIENT ROME

City Planning

From its humble beginnings in the eighth century B.C.E., the city of Rome grew to a power whose empire stretched from the windy tops of Hadrian's Wall in the north of England to the borders of India and south to the Sahara Desert. Roman architecture had a profound influence on both western and eastern Europe that continued for centuries after the empire's destruction in the fifth century C.E.

What made city planning important in ancient Rome was the tremendous population and economic growth the city experienced throughout its history. In ancient Rome, many people lived in poverty in either rural settings or tall tenement housing. Tenements were without sanitation and these homes were a big fire hazard. The cities were big and very crowded. These tenements were built with sloppy plans, wood, and mud bricks. Each time a section of the city burned, therefore, the citizens and leaders made an effort to rebuild on a more logical plan.

Cloaca Maxima

One of the most impressive structures developed by the Romans was the aqueduct and public sewer system. The River Tiber caused some problems for the Romans, since it flooded at regular intervals each year. When the flooding ended, the area submerged would be soaked with stagnant water. Prior to the Romans, the Etruscans, the previous inhabitants of the seven hills on which the city was built, had constructed a trench in an early attempt to drain the marshes. Later known as the Cloaca Maxima, this trench operated as the main sewer in Rome. By the mid-first century B.C.E., Romans were able to capitalize on their new building techniques in order to vault the Cloaca Maxima in stone, allowing it to function as a massive drain to move waste out of the city. The Cloaca Maxima is a true testament to the tremendous foresight of city planners. In fact, the Cloaca Maxima is still the main sewer system in Rome today.

Remove the Mosquitos!

Some scholars believe that the Cloaca Maxima had an even more practical purpose that we can all identify with: get mosquitos out of the area and combat the illnesses that accompany mosquito infestations.

Pont du Gard

Most Romans got their water with buckets from the street fountains, although larger houses might have their own access and system for collecting rainwater from the roof. The fountains worked by gravity, meaning that the weight of the water forced it out of spouts. However, pushing the city's waste into the Tiber made the water unfit for drinking. So the Romans piped in water from fresh springs located outside of Rome. This required a complex system of aqueducts and city reservoirs that used gravity to send water to the city and up through the fountains.

Sometimes the aqueducts needed to cross over valleys and in those cases the Romans used arch support structures to hoist them upward. Some of these stone arches soared as high as 100 feet.

The Pont du Gard in the Roman province of Gaul (today's France) was particularly spectacular, and much of it still survives. Made of unmortared masonry, it rises 160 feet above the valley of River

Gard. It rests on three tiers of arches; the bottom arches are rows of semicircle arches sixty feet in diameter. The span across the river is eighty feet, and the uppermost tier has arches with twenty-foot centers.

Making Concrete

Among the most important contributions of Romans to architecture was the invention of concrete. The Romans developed natural cement as an easier alternative to stone. To make it, they ground pozzolan, a siliceous ash found in volcanic deposits. They then mixed the pozzolan with lime, rubble, and water to make a very hard substance that functioned like stone, even under water. This made architectural work much easier, although it was not nearly as attractive as stone. The Romans used other finishes to cover concrete, materials such as stucco, mosaic, and marble. For the Pantheon in Rome, built in the second century, they used fine, chocolate-red volcanic earth.

Pompeii

Pompeii, near the modern city of Naples, is among the greatest surviving examples of Roman town planning. In C.E. 79, the town was engulfed by an eruption from nearby Mount Vesuvius. The city was filled with ash, lava, and mud, killing thousands of inhabitants. The town remained buried until the eighteenth century; it was first excavated in 1748.

Pompeii was first settled around the sixth century B.C.E.; its early inhabitants included the Greeks, Etruscans, and Samnites. By the time of its destruction it was a resort town, inhabited by 20,000 Romans ranging from wealthy patrician families to middle-class merchants to slaves. Because the eruption was so sudden (the rain of ashes lasted about six hours), death came swiftly and much of the people, animals, and features of the city were preserved in the volcanic ash just as they had been caught.

The town was set up on an irregular grid with oval town walls. It was about 160 square acres in size. The civic center, or the forum, was the center of life in Pompeii. It was marked by a triumphal arch that was both monumental and also served as a barrier to block wheeled vehicles from entering. Inside the forum were the temple to the patron gods of the city, the meat, fish, and vegetable markets, the guild offices, shops, and public lavatories—anything that was at the center of life in Pompeii. Judge offices, council chambers, and various public works were also located here. Public assemblies for legal, commercial, and social purposes were held in the forum as well.

The Roman Forum

Virtually all Roman towns of any size contained forums as their civic focus. The Roman forum eventually became a rectangular plaza that was at the center of Roman life: processions, important speeches, trials, and gladiatorial matches were held here.

Public Baths

Roman baths were used for exercise, relaxation, and also for maintaining hygiene and socializing. There were three baths near the forum at Pompeii. These structures were particularly impressive because it was possible to do so many things in them. There were steam rooms and rooms for cold plunging. Often there were gardens, so it was critical that water supply was consistent and plentiful. Romans even thought of ways to heat the water.

Main Features of the Baths of Diocletian (c.e. 298–306)

- The *caldarium*: an area with hot baths, featuring groin vaulting
- The *tepidarium*: a domed room with warm baths
- The *frigidarium*: a central area with cruciform vaulting designed to accommodate cool baths
- An open-air swimming pool
- Open-air exercise courts

THE ROMAN EMPIRE

Construction Forms

The Romans were masterminds at developing infrastructure. They figured out how to bring clean water into the city and send dirty water out. They developed central heating and the technology to maintain large heated public baths. They built amphitheaters and stadiums where everyone could see a show and the acoustics were fantastic. Romans took architecture beyond post and lintel to adopt compression building, which allowed them to design the arch, vault, and dome. Using these methods, the Romans figured out how to enclose very large spaces. All they needed were modestly sized stones.

Vault Construction

A vault is an arch continued on a longitudinal axis. Post-and-lintel construction is limiting because the supports cannot be too far away from each other. If they are, the lintel, under tension, will crack. Vaulted construction changed everything. Now, the weight could be carried through compression. This meant, though, that the supports had to be much stronger than was necessary with post-and-lintel construction. The upper stone would push downward and outward on the walls or columns below. In order to handle the weight those walls needed to be very thick.

Arch Construction

An arch, in its truest form, is made of wedge-shaped stones (voussoirs) set in a curved shape or a semicircle. Builders would first develop a temporary timber framework called a centering. The voussoirs were laid directly into this centering. This system also made use of a central keystone. Previously, corbeling had been the most popular method used in arch construction. This method involved setting stones on top of each other to create a vaulted or arched shape. Each subsequent stone hangs slightly over the one under it. The stones are built from two sides; as each new course is laid, the shape begins to angle inward until the two sides meet in the middle. Corbeling does not require centering because of the way the stones are securely stacked before two sides meet.

Dome Construction

A dome is an arch that is turned and rotated around its center point. Domes can come in different shapes but they are all formed with vertical lines called meridians and horizontal lines called parallels. The meridians lean in and come together in the center of the arch. These meridians then force the parallels into compression at the top. At the bottom of the dome the meridians push outward, which stretches the parallels to the point of compression.

Vitruvius and *The Ten Books on Architecture*

Much of what we know of early Roman architecture is thanks to Vitruvius (c. 80–c. 15 B.C.E.) and his treatise, *The Ten Books on Architecture*. It is the only surviving book we have on classical building. His work inspired many architects who would follow right into the modern era.

The Pantheon

The Pantheon (C.E. 118–125) is among the best-preserved ancient monuments in Rome. Hadrian, fourteenth emperor of the Roman Empire, was an amateur architect who set out to design something for which he would be remembered. He worked with a team of architects to create a Pantheon, a "temple to the gods." This was intended to replace a crumbling, outdated structure commissioned by Marcus Agrippa in 27 B.C.E.

The new Pantheon was designed with two main parts. First there was a traditional temple entryway with a raised portico, columns, and a triangular pediment. Then there was an innovative circular room covered by a large dome. The exterior has a portico that is only eight columns wide and three deep, so from the outside you would never guess how big this circular room actually is. Workers used a wood scaffold to stand on while they built the walls. Then the concreted dome was poured over a framework placed on them.

The entire building is shaped like a cylinder; a ring of massive piers and large buried arches carry the weight of the dome, which is 143 feet in diameter. These buried arches also distribute the weight around the windows back down to the foundation and piers. At the base, Hadrian used heavy stone called basalt. At the top, he used lightweight volcanic stone called pumice.

Sunken panels called coffers created an attractive geometrical design. These were trapezoidal indentations that appeared in five horizontal rings. Those indentations reduced the weight of the dome. The dome itself is a half-sphere and at the top is a twenty-seven-foot oculus, or skylight, which symbolized a link to the heavens. During the day, the sunshine puts on a show as it casts light around the interior of the structure. At nighttime, it provides a mesmerizing view of the stars. The oculus was placed where the compression forces were the greatest. The builders used a compression ring that was made of a four-and-a-half-inch-thick ring of bricks. The diameter of the dome matches the distance from the oculus to the center floor below perfectly.

The Coliseum

Sports and drama were pillars of Greek and Roman culture. The Romans developed structures that were vaulted so that spectators could watch and everyone could see the action. The amphitheater at Pompeii was oval-shaped. The Theater of Marcellus in Rome was a vaulted semi-circle. The Greeks had previously built their amphitheaters into the hillsides but the Romans created free-standing structures. The Coliseum, or Flavian Amphitheater, in the middle of Rome is the most famous.

In C.E. 64, a devastating fire burned for nine days and destroyed the heart of Rome. When the emperor Nero rebuilt the city, he also rebuilt a giant palace; its compound included an enormous statue of himself, a private park, and a lake closed to the public. He called it the Golden House and the people greatly resented it. Soon there were uprisings and his army went rogue. Things got bad enough that he killed himself.

Following his rule, four emperors reigned who all met early deaths. Vespasian was the new emperor in C.E. 69, and he was desperate to be well liked and avoid the fate of his predecessor. He demolished the Golden House and in its place built a public garden and amphitheater. They renamed the Nero sculpture and called the amphitheater the Coliseum, which was a derivative of "colossus," referring to the huge statute that remained. The Coliseum was built as a great vertical structure to allow all spectators the best view possible. With a height like that, the walls needed to be strong in order to keep the whole thing from collapsing.

Architects drained Nero's lake so that they had a deep area in which to build the foundation of the amphitheater. In the pit they poured a giant ring of concrete in an oval shape, 167 feet wide and forty feet deep. Underground areas were built with heavy concrete and brick. They built the upper levels with wood, bricks, and lighter concrete. Large, decorative, bronze shields hung from the top story of the Coliseum.

Titus, Vespasian's successor and son, opened the Coliseum in C.E. 80. To celebrate, he planned 100 straight days of competition. Titus's brother added another tier during his reign and by C.E. 82 the structure stood 187 feet high and towered over the city.

The Coliseum was oval-shaped and had enough seats for 50,000 people. The plan involved a long ramp that gradually rises as it wraps around the arena until it reaches the top. The top level of seats rested on wooden supports and the rest of the building was made of masonry, a combination of cut stone and concrete. Underneath the seats was a maze of stairs, passageways, and ramps that allowed spectators to get to their seats. The exits and pathways were designed for efficiency in exiting so that everyone could get out in just a few minutes.

The Romans stacked half columns in Doric, Ionic, and Corinthian orders within the building. Arches and supporting barrel vaults created the three-story façade, and the arches carried the weight of the seating. Eighty entrances at the ground level were formed by vaults. These were marked with numbers so that people could easily find their seats. There was even a large canvas that went over the entire structure to shield the interior from the sun and a giant light fixture for nighttime events.

The seats were organized in a hierarchical fashion. The emperor sat in a ground-level marble box with his family and other high-level specta- tors. The next level was the nobles and wealthy citizens. The second tier was the male citizens, while the third tier hosted the women. The high- est tier was standing room for noncitizens and slaves. The floor of the arena was made of wooden sections that could be moved. Underneath were the animal cages that were hoisted up for the competitions.

Gruesome Events at the Coliseum

Coliseum events would open with lighthearted features such as jugglers, ele- phants, and pretend fighting. The emperor would throw colored balls into the audience and those who caught them would win a prize. The Romans brought animals to the arena from all over their empire and hunted them, eliminating many from their habitats (for instance, lions in Mesopotamia).

Gladiator fights themselves were terrible. They would continue until a man was killed or begged for mercy. If the emperor denied his request he was forced to his knees and his throat slit. People dressed as gods would poke fallen gladia- tors with a red-hot iron. If the semiconscious fighter didn't get up he was finished off with a hammer and dragged out of the arena. The sand was raked to get rid of the blood and a new fight began. Eventually, in 404, the gladiator fights were banned, partly due to the crumbling Roman Empire but also because the Christian Church, by then the state religion, denounced the cruelty.

BYZANTINE CHURCHES

The Earliest Houses of Christianity

Christianity was started by the followers of Jesus Christ but did not really start to develop as an organized religion until several hundred years after his death. The Roman Empire had not been terribly welcoming to the Christians but in 313, the emperor Constantine I issued the Edict of Milan, legalizing Christianity. This is when the Christians began openly building churches.

The beginning of the Byzantine era began with the triumph of the emperor Justinian (c. 482–565). Byzantine architecture was distinguished by the use of domes, which were symbols of heaven. Early church styles were eclectic but were generally modeled after Roman temples. (In fact in many cases, the Christians simply took over existing Roman temples.) The result was the Greek-cross plan. This church design included a central square section with four arms of equal length extending from it and a dome roof sitting above the square. A squinch, or arch, was placed in each corner of the square to hold up the dome. Spaces in these churches were huge and decorations were impressive—marble columns, mosaics, and sometimes even gold detailing dazzled worshipers.

Christianity's tenets required that its churches include certain features:

- A table for Communion
- A table for offerings
- Seats for the congregation
- A graveyard (because cremation was not allowed)
- Large spaces capable of holding a lot of people for the processions included in worship services

Basilica of Sant'Apollinare Nuovo

The Basilica of Sant'Apollinare Nuovo in Ravenna was constructed in the early sixth century. The exterior was very plain and made of brick. The interior layout centered on a semicircular apse. Mosaic renderings of Christian stories were included on the ceilings and walls. Christians also built memorials to the saints or martyrs, baptisteries (pools for the purpose of baptizing, a major rite) and mausoleums (tombs for people of note).

Hagia Sophia

Justinian's Hagia Sophia (532–537), or Church of the Divine Wisdom, in Istanbul, Turkey, is one of the most extravagant buildings of all time. It remained the biggest building for nearly 1,000 years and was the place where Byzantine emperors were crowned and the main focus of religious life in Constantinople.

It is, in fact, the third church built on the site. The architects were Anthemius of Tralles and Isidore of Miletus. They divided the space so that the clergy could perform their rituals but there was still enough room for a congregation to watch the service. At the center of the building, the architects constructed four giant limestone supports. These supports, or *piers*, were positioned to form a square and four arches were built on top of them. Within these arches were triangular shapes called pendentives. A pendentive is curved so that it fills the spaces that result when a round ceiling is placed on a square building. In other words, the dome was placed on the arches and the pendentives closed the space that was left between the arches. The dome was made of flat bricks that were laid with thick mortar over wood scaffolding.

Windows that punctured the base of the dome let a lot of light to enter the interior space. Curved ceilings like arches, vaults, and domes are heavy and their weight creates a force that moves outward. This force is called *horizontal thrust*. Additional support is required so that the dome does not crumble under the horizontal thrust. At Hagia Sophia, the builders placed buttresses between the dome windows to reinforce the structure. They used a network of ribs inside the dome for additional strength.

As the interior space stretches out to the east and west sides of the building, two half-domes push up against, or *buttress*, the main dome for additional support. These half-domes are reinforced by semi-domes. All these parts came together to send weight and force to the foundation. Builders included four large rectangular blocks that push up against the main piers to help distribute force and weight in the proper direction. The interior walls beneath the main arches include a number of windows and rows of columns called *colonnades*.

Rebuilding Hagia Sophia

Hagia Sophia is the greatest masterpiece of Byzantine architecture. Twenty years after it was built, though, the church was rocked by a major earthquake. Part of the main dome and one of the semi-domes collapsed. The renovation took on a more hemispherical shape to counteract the tremendous forces on the dome. It turned out the original dome was too shallow to hold all the tension. The new shape was just right and has lasted down to today. The new architect, Isidore the Younger, nephew of one of the original architects, added heavier buttresses and a steeper dome.

ROMANESQUE

The Re-emergence of the City

The Romanesque style was an extension of the Frankish emperor Charlemagne's (c. 742–814) intense campaign to ignite a burst of architecture, design, and style that revived the artistic height of the Roman Empire. Romanesque includes a wide breadth of regional styles that were popular from the tenth through the early thirteenth centuries.

In the early Middle Ages, the feudal system dictated the economic structure and social hierarchy. The center of life was the estate. Now, by the High Middle Ages, trading and commerce started to blossom in the cities. Seaports began to develop along with manufacturing cities and banking centers as well as arts and crafts communities. The cities and towns that had receded into the background during the collapse of the Roman Empire came back to the forefront. Romanesque was the first style that was popular everywhere in western Europe.

Main Features of Romanesque

- Round arches
- Stone vaults
- Relief sculpture
- Thick walls

Regional Names

When Charlemagne died, the Frankish Empire, which included modern-day France, Germany, and Italy, broke apart. In many local areas communities developed but there was no state rule. France, for example, was a loose grouping of subkingdoms united only by the fact that their inhabitants spoke some form of French. For that reason, the names of artistic and architectural styles during this era often are based on specific regions.

Pilgrimages

During the High Middle Ages the church accumulated a lot of wealth, which made it a relatively stable organization. It was able to use that wealth and stability to fund major building projects such as cathedrals and monasteries. Romanesque cathedrals in particular were massive structures using grand features such as Roman vaults and arches. These cathedrals and churches became stops for religious pilgrims as they traveled across Europe.

Pilgrimages were wildly popular (the English poet Geoffrey Chaucer wrote his most famous work, *The Canterbury Tales*, about a group of pilgrims traveling to a holy shrine in Canterbury, England). Devout Christians trekked great distances to churches that housed sacred tokens such as the remains of a saint or a strip of his or her clothing. There were so many pilgrims moving about that architects had to factor them in when building churches, making sure they were allowing enough space to move through the church and observe its relics without disrupting services.

Abbey-Church of Sainte-Foy

The Abbey-Church of Sainte-Foy in Conques, France (c. 1050–1130), was dedicated to a virgin martyr known as St. Faith who had been killed in 305 for refusing to worship pagan gods. The church was fitted with an elaborate gold statue that contained the saint's relics, which attracted hordes of visitors. To accommodate the traffic, architects modified the traditional Latin-cross basilica. The side aisles were extended to form an ambulatory through which lay visitors could walk and view the relics. Now the monks had access to the main altar in the choir without any disruption. Sainte-Foy was among the earliest known pilgrimage churches.

The church was vaulted with transverse ribs that ran across the underside of each quadrant. A second-story gallery was built over the side aisles to accommodate more people. The gallery directed force and weights from the vaults on the side walls back down to the piers of the nave.

The church was distinctly Romanesque in its styling: Sculptures in heavy relief appeared on many of the surfaces such as the tympanum, the arch above at the main entrance; the archivolts; even the trumeau, which was the narrow vertical piece between the front doors.

Romanesque Carving

Romanesque churches were heavily decorated with sculpture. Since the general population could not read, they needed a lot of visual imagery to understand religious stories. Artists also used woven tapestries to tell stories—the tapestries also provided a measure of insulation in the often drafty rooms of churches, castles, and palaces.

The roof of Sainte-Foy was a barrel vault, made of stone, above the nave, lined with arches. Besides eliminating some of the risk of fire, the stone produced magnificent acoustics. These stone vaults were heavy, though, and they required extra support, called buttressing. This construction counteracted the sideways forces of the vault.

Vaulting Systems

A vault is an arch brought forward in space to create a cover over an interior. Vaults were popular in Roman, early Christian, and Byzantine structures, and they experienced a resurgence during the Romanesque period. They were especially popular in church building. Vaults provided fireproofing and they were strong, but they also symbolized the heavens, which soared above man and the earth.

Types of Vaults
- Barrel vaulting: This is the simplest form of vault; an arch is extended to form a semicircular space.
- Groin vaulting: These are created by intersecting two barrel vaults at right angles. The resulting vault is stronger than a barrel vault. A series of groin vaults creates natural divisions between the groins; these divisions are called bays.
- Fan vaulting: In some cases the ribs became wildly elaborate and spread out across the ceiling of the space. Such fan vaults were characteristic of many English cathedrals of the twelfth and thirteenth centuries.
- Rib vaulting: A rib vault is a groin vault to which ribs of stone have been added to the joints, further strengthening the vault.

The Portal

Many pilgrimage churches included carved reliefs above their entrances. The space around the doorways was called a portal. Here the richest reliefs would appear, beckoning visitors to come and worship. Although the architectural structure of portals was similar from church to church, it was the meaning of these images and the stories behind each that distinguished them from one another and drew many visitors.

A Romanesque portal generally included:

- Voussoirs
- Archivolts
- Tympanum
- Lintel
- Jamb
- Trumeau

Pisa

Italian Romanesque buildings were different from those found in France in that they followed the classical Roman tradition to the letter. There were no stylistic innovations like westworks, the great multistory west-facing entrances found on other European Romanesque churches. The Pisans built their cathedral to celebrate a victory against Muslim forces in Sicily. They built their baptistery next door to celebrate a victory against the Christian republic of Amalfi.

The freestanding cathedral at Pisa is elaborate, with double aisles and galleries beside the nave. An oval dome is raised on squinches, and there are shallow pendentives supporting smaller domes. The rest of the church is roofed with wooden trusses. The exterior is sheathed in marble, and rows of columned arcades are stacked upon each other around the building. Inside is found dark and light marble set in a pattern of horizontal bands. There was a circular baptistery, and the apse is decorated in mosaics. (Note that mosaics are more characteristic of Eastern than Western Christian architecture.) The cathedral has a lot of influences: white marble from ancient Rome, floor plan from early Christian basilicas, domes from Islam.

Part of the cathedral complex is the famous Leaning Tower of Pisa. This is the cathedral's bell tower, but because it was built upon unstable ground, even during its construction it began to lean. It is now thirteen feet off its vertical axis. A firmer foundation has been added in modern times to halt the lean.

On the tower, there are six stories of repeated arcaded galleries. This building made an impact and its design style was characteristic of the region for several centuries.

ISLAM
Building the Mosque

Islam originated in 610 in Arabia when the Prophet Muhammad was visited by the angel Gabriel in a cave outside the city of Mecca. By the time Muhammad died in 632 his new religion had spread across Arabia, and over the next few centuries it produced a rich and complex civilization.

Islamic armies took Constantinople in 1453, finally ending the Byzantine Empire. The religion took root in China and India where the Muslims established strong trade networks. Muslims rediscovered many ancient Greek texts, particularly those of Aristotle, and made significant advances in medicine, music, and art. Even though the Christians and the Muslims proved to be adversaries during the Crusades, they developed strong trading relationships through which Islam exercised a profound influence over Europe.

The Islamic empire at its height stretched from Spain to North Africa to Persia and India. By the middle of the sixteenth century, the empire created by the Ottoman Turks was enormous, with strong military and trade and cultural links to Europe.

Islam is based upon five practices: faith, prayer, charity, fasting, and pilgrimage. These practices were intimately linked to the development of a distinctive Islamic architecture.

Development of the Mosque

The earliest mosques were originally created from Christian churches and audience halls used by Persian kings. The Islamic empire was very wealthy; the practice of charity prevented wealthy citizens from saving their fortunes for their descendants. Instead they left their personal wealth for religious, educational, social, and civic purposes. Establishing what were, in effect, charitable foundations required some sort of building complex. These complexes included mosques and were called *kulliyes*. By the end of the second half of the sixteenth century, all great buildings in the Ottoman Empire were either mosques or associated with the kulliyes. An architect named Sinan presided over the construction of most of these structures—nearly 300 structures in Istanbul alone.

Main Features of Ottoman Mosque
- Open prayer hall
- Square prayer hall with a dome
- Portico
- Courtyard surrounded by rows of arches
- One or more minarets

The Dome

Eventually the domed cube became the design used for all buildings in the kulliye. The dome sat on a series of arches built above sturdy columns that surrounded the square interior space. The forces on the dome pushed down and outward. The arches were strong enough to hold the dome but could not counteract these forces. If uncorrected, this would cause the dome to crumble on itself. To combat these forces, architects strengthened the sides of the dome—the area most vulnerable—by adding columns called weight towers at the base of the dome. Using arches instead of solid walls allowed for the space beneath the dome to remain open and airy. To buttress these arches, builders used a series of semi-domes. These two actions worked to send the rest of the dome's hidden forces down the piers to the walls and foundation.

The Kibla

The *kibla* line indicates the direction of Mecca, the holy city of Islam, which is the direction that should be faced during prayer. The kibla wall sits perpendicular to this line and is emphasized by a decorative indentation cut into the wall called the mihrab. The mihrab symbolized the entrance to paradise. Congregants formed rows that were ultimately facing the holy city and its supreme shrine, the Kaaba. The imam positioned himself in front of the mihrab and led everyone in prayer. The main entrance to the prayer hall sat opposite the mihrab. At the center of the building was a *maqsura*, or an enclosed praying area reserved for the sultan or the leader of the mosque. The central section of the mosque where the congregants assembled for services was covered by a wooden dome.

The Sahn

A high portico provided protection above this entrance and overflow space for congregation members. The covered prayer hall is called the *haram*, and was divided into three sections by two parallel rows of columns. Beyond this portico sat a courtyard, called a *sahn*, that was surrounded by arches that sat on top of columns. The passageway formed by these columns is called an arcade. Half of the interior space was used for the arcaded courtyard, which included a domed fountain, called a *sadirvan*, and an octagonal pavilion that contained the treasury. Congregants washed their feet and hands in the sadirvan before entering the prayer hall. The mihrab, entrance, and sadirvan all sat on the kibla line so that they were positioned toward Mecca.

The Minaret

Minaret means "beacon," and minarets were intended as identification for mosques, since they could be seen from a distance, like a bell tower. As well, they were a platform from which the faithful could be called to prayer five times a day. In the first mosques, the minaret stood next to the dome just behind the portico at the northwest corner of the prayer hall. As mosque design progressed many mosques had multiple minarets. The minaret is attached to the mosque and usually has one or more balconies. However, their design varies considerably; they can be spiral, short or tall, skinny or square. Usually the top of a minaret is carved.

CHINA

Thoughtful Planning

Great building projects in China were driven by the government rather than religious or private patrons. The Great Wall of China, one of the mightiest constructions ever undertaken by humans, is a case in point.

The wall, intended to keep the Mongols out of China, began on the northern frontier in the seventh century B.C.E. It continued to be added to through the seventeenth century. In point of fact there were four great walls of China, all of which were intended to protect China from the Mongols and other nomadic tribes to the north.

Phases of the Great Wall of China

- Wall 1 was commissioned by the first emperor of China, Qin Shi Huang (259–210 B.C.E.). It was built by convicts and peasants—hundreds of thousands of workers—and connected a number of existing walls. Today, little of it remains.
- Wall 2 was built by Emperor Han Wudi (156–87 B.C.E.). That was 300 miles long.
- Wall 3 (1138–1198) was an extension about the same length as Wall 2 but it ran in the opposite direction, leading from the eastern end of the Great Wall at Shanhaiguan and snaking its way north to Dandong on the Yalu River.
- Wall 4 (1368–1644) is the best-known and best-preserved of the walls. It began during the reign of the first emperor of the Ming Dynasty, Zhu Yuanzhang (1328–1398). The building continued until the fall of the last Ming emperor in 1644. By the end, the wall was about 4,000 miles long.

Those who presided over the wall's construction e
sized the importance of using local materials and tra
struction. The eastern half of the wall is made of dre
kiln-fired brick. The western half is made of pise (
Sometimes that section was dressed with sun-dried brick. The wan
included a series of watchtowers, gateways, and forts so it could be
staffed with troops of soldiers.

Eventually the Mongols in 1449 and the Manchus in 1664 got
through the wall. The Manchus established themselves in Beijing as
the ruling dynasty. After that the Great Wall was no longer used as
a major defense but continued to be a national symbol and a monument to the men and women who built it. Many died in the process,
and it has been said that their bones are interred in the wall.

Taoism and Confucianism

Lao Tzu and Confucius were the most influential Chinese religious figures. Lao
Tzu (c. sixth century B.C.E.) founded the discipline of Taoism, which seeks a
means for achieving harmony between man and the world. Taoist principles
were especially evident in landscape design. Confucius (c. 551–479 B.C.E.) was
more concerned with respect for authority. Those in authority are supposed
to act benevolently toward their subjects. His teachings emphasized ancestor
worship and respect for one's family. City planning and home design in China
have been based on Confucian principles.

Planning According to Cardinal Direction

In Chinese architecture, the way buildings are placed points to
Confucian and Taoist teachings. Cardinal directions play a major
role in orientation. There is a kind of a hierarchy followed here:

the most important buildings and homes face south where they take maximum sun. This also offers some protection from the winds.

- Secondary buildings face east or west. These are often protected by overhangs on the structure or even trees and shrubs.
- Architectural plans honor Taoist ideas about living harmoniously with nature.

Feng Shui

Feng shui, or the art of creating harmony with the environment is an extension of Taoist principles. Meaning "wind and water," feng shui sees these two elements in constant interaction with one another. It is a mystical practice that combines many cultural traditions with ancient wisdoms. Feng shui presents a set of principles for the design and layout of interior and exterior spaces. The practice is intended to develop a harmonious relationship with nature, which in turn translates to harmony between domestic partners and families. All of this contributes to good health and prosperity. Practitioners believe firmly that if you ignore these laws you will meet unhappiness, bad health, and even lose money.

Here are some main principles:

- Tall buildings with sharp angles and edges produce bad energy. Instead, use rounded corners.
- You must consider the size of the door so that it is not too big or too small in relation to the building. No sharp objects should face the door. If something like that cannot be helped, use mirrors to reflect them away.

A feng shui master works alongside an architect or engineer throughout the process of building. To be successful at feng shui, you need to become an expert in topography so that you can understand the earth and, therefore, how to properly organize spaces to maximize good chi and minimize the bad. Chi is universal energy. Good, well-balanced chi is cosmic breath. Dad, defective chi is killing breath. True believers actually say that Buckingham Palace is poorly positioned because the building faces a long straight road and the front court has no plants.

Jian

The basic modular unit of any Chinese building is called a *jian*. A jian measures about ten feet by fifteen feet. The simplest homes might measure a single jian. Bigger buildings can have multiple jians, with care to make sure there are an odd number. Using an odd number ensures that one jian can act as the exact middle or the center of the home. Larger buildings would involve rooms that were treated almost as separate structures, connected to one another by corridors. These allow for separate units, containing areas for different functions.

Temples

Buddhism was the most widespread religion in China, and the most popular structure for Buddhist worship was the temple complex. This included a hall for viewing (venerating) the images of Buddha, and a separate pagoda. The pagoda was inspired by the finials that topped stupas in northern India as well as by multistoried watchtowers favored by the Chinese military. It was a multistory building with multiple roofs—one for each level. Pagodas were built to store relics and sacred writings but their vertical stature also allowed them to stand out as landmarks, showing where the temple was located. Roofs were propped up by large wooden brackets connected to main structure. These brackets, called *dougong*, interlocked with the columns of the building frame and crossbeams of the roof. These brackets also strengthened the walls, which allowed for taller structures.

Cave temples in northern India were inspired by the same structures. These caves were cut into steep cliffs during the fifth and sixth centuries. The ornamentation features many things found in India: elephants, lotus plants, and swirling vines.

Secular Buildings

With the exception of the watchtower and pagoda, most Chinese buildings were horizontally laid out and not more than one story tall. Important buildings were built atop platforms so that they sat a little higher than the other structures. These buildings were also larger and boasted more decorative aspects such as hipped roofs that were supported by brackets. Generally, Asian buildings were decorated in far brighter colors than their Western counterparts. Buildings of lesser importance were smaller with gabled roofs, and were usually decorated with plain colors such as brown and black. Most Chinese buildings were organized around courtyards and in most cases were built of wood. Ceramic casts of homes found in Han dynasty burials lend us some knowledge about the kinds of houses that were built; this is fortunate, since the wooden versions did not survive the ravages of time.

JAPANESE ARCHITECTURE

A Flexible Style

Japan's early architecture was influenced by neighboring China. Like China, it was also influenced by Buddhism. The earliest surviving Japanese structures were built with a post-and-lintel system and held in place with elaborate brackets.

In Japan, wood was always the primary building material because it was readily available. Bamboo, the primary wood used, is strong, flexible, and extremely easy to manipulate in building. This was an important point in a country regularly ravaged by earthquakes. The sort of heavy bracing or masonry techniques developed in western Europe would have collapsed during a severe quake. Bamboo, on the other hand, absorbed the shock.

However, wooden buildings often decay or burn down. There are not many surviving structures from ancient Japan. Let's take a look at what we know.

Shinto

Called the way of the gods, this is the native religion of Japan. It is focused on a series of rituals carried out throughout the year and is polytheistic. It celebrates natural forces associated with agriculture. As it grew, it overlapped with Buddhism.

Shinto Shrines

Shinto shrines were built as temporary structures. Followers believed that gods would only visit the earth for short periods at a time, so they didn't require permanent structures. Even today, Shinto shrines are completely rebuilt at twenty-year intervals. When a new emperor's reign began, a new castle was built to ensure its purity. Many of the Shinto structures have been replaced many times—though each is an exact replica of what came before it.

Domestic Architecture

In ancient Japan, the streets were lined with single-story row houses interspersed with bustling storefronts. These buildings were constructed with wooden posts that sat on stones, creating a foundation. The roofs were gabled and built with planks. There were earthen floors throughout but one room was usually set on a raised wooden floor. A lightweight material called wattle and daub was used to plaster the walls. Wattle and daub involves a latticework wattle made of wooden strips that are then covered with a substance made of wet soil, clay, sand, grass or straw, and even animal dung. Street-facing windows were placed high in the walls to deter voyeurs. Japanese summers are often humid, and much consideration was given to maximizing air circulation. Houses were built on platforms and interior spaces fitted with sliding screens that could be opened to let in a breeze. Overhangs and roofs provide shade in the summer but let the winter sunlight get in. These overhangs also send rain away from the house. Later, elaborate tiled roofs became popular for large buildings.

Early wooden houses, called *minka,* had areas in which animals were stabled that were not separated from the rooms in which the families lived (this was true of family dwellings in western Europe as well). There was also usually a hearth area on an earth floor and a sleeping area with a raised wooden floor. Gabled roofs with vents allowed hearth smoke to exit the home. The gables were covered on the outside with thatch or even wooden shingles to protect from rain and snow. These homes contained minimal furniture and a simplicity that lent itself to flexibility. The rooms could easily be adapted for multiple functions by moving things around or rolling up a bed.

Zen Buddhism

Zen Buddhism originated in China and came to Japan in the twelfth century when contact between the two societies expanded. It became widely popular in Japan and influenced the development of the country's architecture. Zen emphasizes enlightenment through meditation.

Zen Buddhist Temples

Zen Buddhist temples are complexes and much more elaborate than Shinto shrines. The focal point is the main worship hall containing a statue of the Buddha. Columns that support the roof are made of wood. The eaves of these buildings are less pronounced than on dwellings, which emphasizes the structure's horizontal lines. Instead of ornate, external brackets, the roof supports are positioned under the ceiling beams where they are largely hidden from view.

Zen meditation requires tremendous concentration and these spaces were created to encourage this among the monks. The buildings have a bilateral symmetry and the components inside are organized in a simple, predictable format so that nothing distracts the worshiper. The roof is steeply angled at the top and ornamented with decorated eaves. As the roof descends, it tapers off into a gentler angle. The temples' design flows easily into the natural scenery.

The Buddhist temple complex Hōryū-ji in Nara, Japan (seventh century), some of the oldest wooden buildings in the world, include a pagoda, a wooden temple, a cloister temple, quarters where the monks lived, and a gate. The entire complex was organized on an east-west axis and is nestled in a valley so that the landscape provides a natural fence or enclosure. It also included a *kondō*, or sanctuary hall, called the Golden Hall. The proximity of the pagoda and the kondō, which face each other, creates a balance because they are asymmetrical structures.

Teahouses

Another important tradition in Japanese culture is the tea ceremony. Tea originated in China but once its popularity spread to Japan it became a ritual in the Zen tradition. Teahouses are usually constructed away from other buildings, in isolated locations. They appear suddenly at the end of paths, giving them an air of discovery. Teahouses are built to look like an extension of nature, they are rustic with a lot of wood elements and an irregular frame. Doorways are extremely low. Windows are low enough that when one is seated they appear at eye level.

Teahouses are designed to be harmonious, tranquil spaces where guests can reflect and attain internal simplicity and calm. There is intentionally no main focal point. A tea room is relatively small, about twelve and a half feet by twenty-five feet, big enough to contain several traditional rice straw mats, called tatami. The room is tidy, small, and simple. Visitors leave their shoes outside. Teahouses are good examples of how the aesthetics of early Shinto shrines and the principles of Zen Buddhism came together in Japanese architecture.

Tatami

Although tatami come in different sizes, depending on the area of Japan where they are made, they are always constructed so that the length is exactly twice the width. Rules were put in place in different epochs concerning the number of tatami permitted in a room and how they should be arranged. An inauspicious tatami arrangement was said to bring ill fortune to a house.

Katsura Imperial Villa

The Katsura Imperial Villa (1620–1663) was a palace complex of individual villas in Kyoto, Japan, built over three generations of the Hachija-no-Miya family during the seventeenth century. It was a country house intended for noble citizens and warriors to come take little vacations for reflection and relaxation. This is a big place whose interior spaces were constructed according to precise rules regarding tatami mats. There were many open porches from which the inhabitants could view and contemplate nature.

The buildings' structural frame was made of Japanese cedar wood, called *hinoki*. The rooms were separated by wooden doors or paper-covered partitions. These partitions could be moved, like sliding doors, in order to open up spaces and change the dimensions of the interior rooms. The grounds include extensive gardens and a lake. These serve as the main ornamentation for the villa because the structure itself is austere. The decks and porches are built as extensions of the interior space.

Japanese Sliding Doors (Shoji Doors)

Shoji doors are made of translucent paper fastened over a wood frame. The frame keeps together a latticework of wood or bamboo construction. The traditional paper used in these doors is called *washi*. In houses and other buildings where space is at a premium, shoji take up less space than doors that swing.

RUSSIAN ARCHITECTURE
New Christianity

The Byzantine basilica gained attention in Russia in 988 when Prince Vladimir of Kiev converted from paganism to Christianity. He did his research before converting and studied the ritual faiths of all the major Western religions, inviting representatives from Judaism, Islam, Latin Christianity, and Greek Christianity to come visit him and tell him about their faiths. Then he sent his own people to church services all around the world to investigate what they were like. In the end, his people were so impressed with Hagia Sophia that they wrote in their journals, "We know not whether we are in heaven or on earth."

Vladimir embraced Eastern Christianity . . . for the architecture as much as for its religious beliefs. Missionaries came from Constantinople to help Vladimir create a Christian culture in Russia; this included translating the Bible, building schools, and erecting churches.

Saint Sophia Cathedral

When Christianity first appeared in Russia, Kiev was the center of government and culture. Vladimir's son Yaroslav the Wise presided over the building of Saint Sophia in Kiev, the first church built there. While it was inspired by Hagia Sophia in Constantinople, the Russian builders did not have the technology or knowledge to make something as enormous. Instead of one gigantic dome, they improvised and made multiple domes over small interior spaces positioned next to one another. The main plan of the church is a quincunx, and a Greek cross defines the central space. The interior is vaulted and the plan is organized around this central area. There is a major dome in the middle but twelve additional domes are set on high drums at varying levels. Additional arcading was added later along with two large circular towers that hold staircases on either side.

The church was damaged in 1240 and left as a ruin for hundreds of years. In the seventeenth and eighteenth centuries there was an effort to rebuild and restore it but with a Baroque style. The building we see today looks completely different from the original version.

The Church of the Nativity of the Virgin

Wood was the dominant Russian building material until the twentieth century. It was readily available and very easy to work with. The style of building in the country was often similar to the American log cabin with horizontal logs, and notches into which the next layer of logs would fit. Americans usually built wooden structures as temporary shelter until they were able to develop something more attractive and impressive. Russians, however, kept their wood structures for a long time. Entire cities were often built from wood. Not surprisingly, fires were common.

The Great Fire of Moscow

In 1812 the French emperor Napoleon invaded Russia. Meeting only weak resistance, he drove the Russian troops back until in September he entered Moscow. The Russians abandoned their capital city and, by some accounts, set parts of it on fire. The flames raged for six days, destroying three-quarters of Moscow. Napoleon's inability to stop the destruction of many valuable supplies contributed to the disaster his army underwent as it left Moscow and retreated along the long road back to France.

Wooden churches usually had high gable roofs so that they would be visible in the landscape. The floors were raised off the ground at least one story to accommodate the winter snow. In a land known for its freezing temperatures, the weather had an influence on Russian building styles. The Church of the Nativity of the Virgin (1117–1119) at Peredki had an external covered passage, called a *gallery,* wrapped around the building. Stacked cantilevers, called *pomochi*, extended out from the main walls and supported the gallery from underneath. This protected visitors in the snow. Birch bark covered the areas where the roof intersected with walls. Builders made shingles out of aspen and placed them in interesting patterns, not least because they would age nicely in cold weather. The roof boards were pointed at the ends to guide water away from the roof.

The Church of the Transfiguration in the Republic of Karelia in Russia was an especially extended version of this church. It is a Greek-cross plan made of wood with twenty-two domes. Aspen shingles topped the gables which were placed with a reverse curve known as a *bochki*. The domes appear on drums that are not very wide and the composition comes together in a pyramid shape. One large dome sits at the top, four in the middle, and eight on the lowest story. Over the arms of the Greek-cross plan are two more sets of four domes. The bochki were decorated with shingles that had been cut to have decorative edges, which also help with directing away water. The aspen has aged to a silver that looks almost metallic, and glints.

The inside of the building is nowhere near as grand as the exterior. The ceilings are not nearly as high as one would think and the main attraction is the icons.

The Onion Dome

In the Russian architectural tradition, onion domes are believed to have symbolized burning candles. When they appear in groups of three they represent the Holy Trinity; in groups of five they represent Jesus and the four evangelists. A single onion dome is said to symbolize Jesus.

Saint Basil's Cathedral

Eventually, wooden construction was replaced by masonry covered with colorful tiles and bricks. Saint Basil's Cathedral (1555–1561), officially the Cathedral of the Intercession of the Virgin on the Moat, located on Red Square in Moscow is today the pride of the Russian Orthodox Church and a top tourist destination. It was built right outside of the Kremlin's walls as a celebration of Ivan IV's victory at the siege of Kazan in 1552. The design is a central plan with nine separate chapels and eight domes, representing the eight attacks on Kazan. Four of them are large and octagonal in size and four cover smaller, square chapels. A ninth dome was added in 1588 for Basil's tomb. This dome is green and gold and decorated with small gold pyramids. The sanctuary is covered by a tall roof.

The other chapels have domed towers, each with a slightly different treatment from the other. Additional external elements include galleries and stairs, all covered. The structure contains multiple gables, some in semicircular shapes and others in triangular forms. The roofs are covered with glazed tiles in a variety of presentations such as zigzags and spirals and stripes. The exterior is trimmed with red brick and white stone. Inside, winding galleries connect the chapels, and stairways make all the levels accessible.

Napoleon Green with Envy

Legend says that Napoleon was completely obsessed with this church. In 1812, after successfully invading Russia and reaching Moscow, he wanted to take it back to Paris with him but could not figure out how to do it so he ordered that it be destroyed. The French under his command had their kegs of gunpowder lit and ready when a sudden unexpected rain put out their fuses, saving the cathedral.

For centuries, religious buildings were the main type of public architecture in Russia. They were also, for many years, the only buildings that were built of masonry, so they tend to be the only buildings that survived the ravages of time.

MONASTERIES

Centers of Learning

Monasteries provided some of the most impressive architecture of the Middle Ages. Monks took a vow of poverty and isolation as a means to get closer to God. The first Christian monastery was founded in the early fourth century in Egypt but St. Benedict founded a monastery at Monte Cassino, Italy, in the sixth century that established the structure we are most familiar with. By the middle of the twelfth century, there were 500 monasteries in England alone.

St. Benedict

Benedict was one of the founding fathers of the monastic movement, particularly for his Rule, which codified monastic practices that had grown up over the centuries. The Benedictine monks took a strict vow of poverty, chastity, and obedience, dividing their day into religious services, physical labor, and the copying of religious manuscripts. The Frankish emperor Charlemagne ordered all monasteries in his region to follow the Rule of St. Benedict. Monasteries were part of Charlemagne's strategy for controlling the territories that he had conquered.

Benedict's Rule became the main mode for monasteries and also convents throughout Europe. Before a potential monk took his vows he was asked to spend a year living at a monastery to make absolutely certain that it was the right choice for him. At the point that he took his vows, he shaved the crown of his head in what was called a tonsure, said to be an imitation of Christ's crown of thorns.

Monks tended to be well educated. Charlemagne decreed that monasteries needed to provide education even to those not intending to take holy orders. Monasteries were known as places that put a high premium on education, and for this reason an important part of the monastery was the library, to which was attached the scriptorium, where holy books were written or copied. Some of the books that modern historians have relied on to learn more about the Middle Ages came out of monasteries; St. Bede, a monk at the northern English monasteries of Wearmouth and Jarrow, wrote the *Ecclesiastical History of the English People*, a seminal work in our understanding of the history of early England. Monasteries were ruled by abbots, and convents were run by abbesses.

Entering a holy order at one of these establishments was a life commitment. Monks and nuns spent their days attending worship services, reading, teaching, and caring for the poor. They also had to tend to the monastery's land, which might include a farm, garden, and ponds. These activities allowed the monasteries to become self-sustaining, and with time some monasteries grew extremely wealthy, owning great tracts of land.

Monks and nuns were expected to take in travelers and care for anyone sick, so their buildings needed to accommodate others beside themselves. Much was included within the walls: latrines, an infirmary, a cloister (a covered walkway surrounding an open courtyard), a water tower, a herbarium, a church, a refectory (where the monks ate), a chapter house (or dormitory), and a cemetery. The monastery functioned like a small town. Many monks became experts in specific arts or crafts.

Charlemagne did much to encourage construction of rural monasteries during the Middle Ages, and by the tenth century, the general architectural structure of the monastery had been established.

The church was the largest building, a double-ended basilica, usually with masonry walls and a timber truss roof. Often it needed to include multiple altars to honor individual saints. Whenever possible, as with other Christian churches, the monastic church was oriented along an east-west axis, with the altar on the eastern end. The westwork referred to the towers and other decorative elements on the western end of the church, which was its primary entrance.

Branching off from the church were the other buildings of the monastery, grouped around a central square, or cloister. A cloister had four covered walkways that bordered it. Often, the monastery's herb garden was located in the center of the cloister. To that end, it was often placed at the south side of the church, with maximum exposure to the sun. As well, the scriptorium, where the monks copied manuscripts, was placed where it would receive the greatest natural light. The cloister was, effectively, the heart of the monastery. The columns that supported its walkway roofs often included capitals that were covered with sculptures telling stories from the Bible.

To remove the monks from temptation, monasteries were usually built in remote places. The monks searched for a place with a good water supply and land that could be tilled. In many cases, as monasteries settled and grew in size, secular communities sprang up around them.

In 1098 a group of monks, led by Robert, abbot of Molesme, split away from the Benedictines and formed their own order, the Cistercians. These monks sought even more remote areas in which to build monasteries and were responsible for settling previously unpopulated parts of Europe, particularly France. Cistercian buildings were plain but elegant and had no stained windows, reflecting their concern for austerity. The Cistercians were reacting against the wealth that the Benedictines were amassing.

Lorsch Abbey Gatehouse

The Abbey of Lorsch was among those commissioned by Char-lemagne, but today only the ninth-century gatehouse (Torhalle) remains. It is, however, a powerful testament to the heavy Roman influence on Carolingian architecture. The ground level boasts a row of triumphal arches. Between each arched entrance is a Corinthian column. Second-floor windows are surrounded by triangular frames. Here are the Carolingian aspects of the structure: a steeply pitched roof (that sheds the rain and snow of northern European winters) and decorative red and white tiles (made by local artisans).

Destruction of the Monasteries

In 1534, in a religious revolution Henry VIII broke from the Catholic Church and declared himself head of the Church of England. As part of this action and to gain badly needed wealth, he seized the lands belonging to English monasteries and dissolved them. By the time of Henry's death in 1547, monasteries in England had effectively ceased to exist.

NATIVE PEOPLE OF NORTH AMERICA

Portable Lifestyle

For the native people of North America, architecture was viewed as a means for sheltering people as well as a symbolic representation of their position between the earth and the sky. North America is large with an extremely diverse environment. The people of each region found ways to build on the land so that the style of architecture fit their needs. The tribes of the Great Plains and Great Lakes were nomadic so their domestic architecture was portable. They created structures that could be quickly assembled with materials that could be reused. In the Southwest, structures were more permanent, sometimes carved from earth or developed into areas that provided natural protection.

Tipi

The tribes of the great plains preferred a portable home called the tipi. In these places tribes followed the migrations of animals on which they relied for food and a variety of other things, including shelter. The Arapaho, Blackfoot, Cheyenne, Comanche, and Crow all preferred these portable homes. The tipi could be adjusted to accommodate hot or cold weather and protect from rain or wind. Tribesmen fashioned a collection of poles into a cone. Then, bison hides were fitted over the frame to form the walls. Having sealed walls also ensured that the fire the inhabitants kindled inside would not go out; the smoke escaped through a hole at the top of the tipi.

Tipis were simple but were remarkable structures. For additional protection from wind, inhabitants could push the tipi down to flatten the shape. The bison hides could be pulled back to allow for ventilation during the hot summer months. The bison hides were sometimes decorated with painted murals that represented dreams or spiritual traditions.

Tipis were not necessarily single-family dwellings. Some were so big that it took thirty bison hides to cover them. When the tribes moved, the tipi could be collapsed and dragged behind the horses.

The Wickiup

The wickiup, or wigwam, was popular in the northeast and in some areas of the northwestern plains. These structures involved a structure similar to the tipi. Saplings were driven into the ground and bent over to form a dome at the top. The curved framework of the wickiup was covered with smaller saplings and thatch or large pieces of bark. The domed shape helped the wickiup stay sturdy in wind and bear heavy loads of snow. These homes were usually about 15–20 feet wide.

Earth Lodges

A number of tribes in the Great Plains and Eastern Woodlands built earth lodges. This was a post-and-lintel configuration of logs. Builders dug a few feet below the surface to establish the foundation, which also meant that the floor sat below ground level. This ensured that the logs were sturdy when set in the ground. Poles leaned against the logs to form a conical shape, and the walls were formed by packing earth over the framework. Buildings used the wattle-and-daub technique for smearing the earth. This layer of earth provided strong insulation against extreme temperatures, such as one finds at the height of winter and summer. The Navajos in the southwest lived in hogans. Hogans were built by stacking logs or poles in a circular fashion, leaving an open space for a doorway. These stacks would rise as the walls and then curve over to make a ceiling which was in the shape of a dome. The gaps between the stacks were filled with leaves and sticks and the entire structure was covered with mud.

Earth Lodge Labor

Women played a major role in constructing tipis and earth lodges. Two women would work together to raise a tipi. With the earth lodges, men constructed the big logs for posts and lintels but the women did the rest of the work. For that reason, these structures were considered to be owned by women, and ownership of these homes was passed through the female line. Men needed to ask for permission from a woman before adding any decoration to their homes.

Cahokia

Cahokia (c. C.E. 800–c. late 1300), near the city of St. Louis, was the largest city north of Mexico and was likely the origin of Mississippian culture. The Cahokia culture was a grouping of agricultural communities that stretched from the American Midwest to the Southeast. The settlement itself was about five square miles with a population at its height of 30,000.

Platform mounds were popular in Cahokia and built in a layout that functioned like a city. These mounds can be found in many other parts of the Midwest and South. Some of them were very advanced; in fact at least one of these structures was ten stories high. Monks Mound, the most famous, was located in what is now central Alabama, and was made of earth. This site is shaped like a pyramid.

Learning about Cahokia

Learning about Cahokia and its culture has proven to be a difficult task. The Cahokia tribe had no written language. To make matters worse, European settlers were intent on suppressing these cultures and were largely successful.

Shed Houses

Shed houses were popular in the Northwest. Here, tribes such as the Quinault survived off plants, fish, and sea mammals. Builders used circular beams to construct the log frames for shed houses. They then sheathed these frames with cedar planks. Cedar bark ties held the parts in place, and the structures were topped with gabled roofs.

Pit Houses and Other Shelters

The Yakima constructed timber frames in post-and-lintel construction above three- to four-foot pits to build pit houses. They used pine needles, earth, and grass mats to cover these frames. Members of the Pima tribes made ki houses. Saplings formed a dome-shaped frame in a shallow pit. A kiva was a circular pit that contained a space for social and ceremonial events. Each kiva included a *sipapu*, an opening to the spirit world below.

Ramadas were warm-weather homes. Builders planted posts in the ground and then built a roof out of brush above them.

Pueblos

Southwestern tribes built pueblos. These began as pit houses but evolved into houses that were positioned at the ground level. Pueblo houses had timber floors that were topped with earth. One entered them through a hole at the top. The builders used sandstone as masonry and small timbers for roofs. They topped the roofs with adobe. Eventually pueblos became so advanced that they included multiple stories and functioned as full housing complexes. One of the most famous housing systems, Mesa Verde, was built in an area under a huge cliff that acted as a natural shelter.

Bison

At the peak of their existence, about 60 million bison grazed from the east to the west coast of North America. For many tribes, the bison was the center of their culture. The animals' bones served as tools like knives and sewing needles, hides for shelter, blankets, clothing, and meat for nourishment. The coming of white men disrupted all this; within less than a century, hunters had slaughtered nearly 50 million of the creatures. It took much of the twentieth century to bring the animals back from near-extinction.

EARLY GOTHIC

Cathedral Building

The Gothic style of architecture was popular from the twelfth to the sixteenth centuries in Western Europe. The name itself was initially an insult. "Gothic" refers to the Germanic tribes who wreaked havoc on western Europe in the fourth century, invading Italy and toppling the Roman Empire. Goths destroyed much of classical civilization, and when in the sixteenth century the critic Vasari wrote that the architecture of the High Middle Ages was "Gothic," he was saying it was the kind of thing that might have been erected by barbarians.

From the twelfth century on, many cathedrals were built throughout Europe. A cathedral is the seat of a bishop (the word *cathedral* comes from the Latin *cathedra*, meaning "seat"). During the early Gothic period, urban centers were beginning to grow. Cathedral building was both a consequence of and a contribution to that population shift and ensuing social developments. Building a cathedral created many jobs for artists and craftsmen. Once a cathedral was finished, it attracted thousands of pilgrims, who would spend money in the town on their visit. People were very proud of their cathedrals.

Abbot Suger

Abbot Suger, born c. 1081, was educated at the monastery school of Saint-Denis. He studied with the future French king Louis VI and they kept in touch when school ended. When they grew up,

King Louis VI asked Suger to serve as his political adviser to his son, the future Louis VII. Suger's job required him to run interference between the church and the royal family. He did a good job and in 1122, Suger was appointed as the abbot of Saint-Denis. This was a great honor because St. Denis was the patron saint of France and the royal family's burial plot was held there.

The original Carolingian church at Saint-Denis was built in the eighth century. Now its leader, Suger decided to make it bigger and better. He spent years researching and planning. He was particularly inspired by the biblical account of the building of Solomon's Temple. He read what he believed were the writings of St. Denis (historians now believe that he was actually reading the work of Pseudo-Dionysius, a mystic theologian of the fifth or sixth century). He was completely transfixed by the author's narratives on the importance of well-positioned light on a building and the mathematical proportions that should exist between a building's parts. The author of these texts emphasized complete harmony in architecture.

The more he read, the more Suger became obsessed with light. He was not just thinking about the design impact of light but also the symbolism and what it implied about Christ and his divine presence. When Suger planned his building, he used existing medieval styles but he switched everything around to emphasize the light. He wanted to express God's presence. When he was finished making these adjustments, the effect was revolutionary.

First he added a new narthex, or covered porch, at the west end of the building. There was a west-facing façade with twin towers, which included three portals. He kept the interior open so that pilgrims could walk about without disturbing the clergy. But he covered the nave with ribbed vaults and pointed arches. Then, he used slender columns to support the arches, which made everything seem even lighter. This was a departure from the dark and heavy mood of the Romanesque churches. He placed thin buttresses between the chapels on the outside of the building to strengthen the walls (these came to be called flying buttresses). The practical impact of these changes was to make the church walls thinner and higher. Suger now removed large sections of the walls and replaced them with stained glass.

The effect was to fill the interior of the church with light—but not ordinary light. This was light that had been transformed by its passage through the stained-glass images into a symbol of the presence of God. The whole purpose of this new architectural style was to emphasize this transformed light. Suger's Saint-Denis is the first example of Gothic architecture.

People were immediately captivated by the building, which looked so different from the massive Romanesque cathedrals. The style became a runaway hit in France and was copied all over the country. It soon spread to England, Spain, and Germany. Italy was the most reluctant to adopt the look, and the Italian Gothic period did not last as long as that of other areas.

Vaults

The vaults at Saint-Denis show that something new is going on with Suger's design. The ribbed vault requires less buttressing than the stone barrel vaults that were prevalent in Romanesque churches. Barrel vaults were formed by a series of arches that stretched a horizontal distance like a long hall, for example. These simple but heavy vaults put pressure on the entire length of the structure. The groin vault was an innovation on the simple barrel vault system because it brought together two barrel vaults to make an angular dome over a larger indoor space like a market. The groin vault sends weight to the corners of the four bays formed beneath the dome. Since the weight is absorbed by the bays, there is no need for a wall to support the roof. Corner buttresses can support the structure instead. The ribbed vault distributes pressure the same way but, instead of buttresses, ribs in the ceiling ensure that the weight is sent to the corners of the bays. All that extra space that is not covered by a buttress can now be punctured with windows.

Once compound piers started appearing between wall openings in Gothic churches, vaults became even more complex. Compound piers have two supports coming from the same base. These double supports made it possible to bring the rib lines all the way down to the floor by colonnettes that rested on them, almost like trees. The combination of the double piers, ribs, and repeating colonnettes created a vertical uniformity that drew attention to the amazing windows.

Flying Buttresses

In the Gothic style, builders aimed to get rid of the thick walls that had buttressed Romanesque structures. The flying buttress was the perfect solution. It used additional free-standing arches to brace the walls and reinforce the points of the vault that were most vulnerable to pressure. Vaults endure the most stress at the top and where they curve. The intent of the flying buttress is to push the downward forces into the curve of the vault and into the wall below it. These innovations, which resembled half-arches attached to the walls, become a notable feature on the exteriors of many Gothic cathedrals.

Ribs

Pointed arches can be wider or narrower stylistically; those variations are difficult to achieve with rounded arches. In pointed arches,
piers channel the thrust of the pointed arch downward. No matter
how close or how far apart their supports are, they can be raised to
any height. This enabled Suger and his successors to stretch the vertical lines of their buildings.

Types of Ribs

- Unifying rib: Ribs have a shaft on the nave piers. This unites the vault with the arcade.
- Sexpartite: Each bay of the vault is divided into six sections by intersecting ribs.
- Quadripartite: Each bay is divided into four sections by the intersecting ribs.
- Ridge rib: There are a lot of ridge ribs: ribs over the windows and intermediate ribs. Intermediate ribs are called tierceron ribs.
- Lierne vaulting: Decorative ribs that are not structurally engaged.
- Net vaulting: Rib configuration used only to create surface design.

Stained Glass

Before Suger, stained glass had appeared here and there but in Gothic architecture, it became an essential feature in religious buildings. Tracery is the stonework that supports and decorates stained-glass windows. In plate tracery, the stone infilling is thick, dominating the window. Bar tracery is much thinner and delicate, so there is more glass than stonework. Tracery required the work of an incredibly gifted stone mason.

More Concern for Mary

Gothic cathedrals emphasized the Virgin Mary in Christian worship. They depicted her as begging Christ to be lenient in his judgment of humanity. Impassioned and life-like images of Mary appeared frequently in stained-glass and sculpture as a way to allure Christians.

HIGH GOTHIC

Confidence in a Style

By the time of High Gothic style, builders had refined their techniques and polished the components to convey symmetry and unity. The design emphasis was on light and height. Medieval architects determined how to place the elements of the walls to draw the eye upward and maximize the height and the light as it soaked through the clerestory, the line of windows just below the roof. The term *High Gothic* refers to the time when Gothic style reached its highest point of development. It marks a decisive break with the older, heavier Romanesque style.

Chartres Cathedral

Among the finest cathedrals built during the High Gothic period was the Cathedral of Notre-Dame at Chartres (1194–1220), commonly known as Chartres Cathedral. This site was an important stop for pilgrims for a long time because it housed what was believed to be a tunic worn by Mary, mother of Jesus. The first structure built on the site was destroyed by a terrible fire. Its replacement, a Romanesque basilica, caught fire again, which caused great damage to the westwork. The replacement, borrowed from Saint-Denis, was a west façade with three portals. The stained glass was also inspired by the panels at Saint-Denis, which depicted stories such as the passion and the birth of Jesus.

Tragically, in yet another fire the old basilica was completely destroyed, as was most of the surrounding city. The people were devastated. They took it as a sign of God's unhappiness with them.

As they sifted through the rubble, they realized that the case with Mary's tunic had survived the fire. They were thrilled and took it as a sign from Mary that she wanted a bigger church. They spent the next twenty-six years rebuilding the church, transforming it into a structure to please her. They kept the crypt of the old structure and maintained the west façade that had survived the destruction. This time, they used the Gothic style and made an enormous clerestory window.

Parts of a Gothic Church

High Gothic churches included the following features:

- Arcade: An arcade is a series of arches that are supported by piers or columns. There is typically a passageway between the arches and a solid wall or a covered walkway. Some arcades support a wall or a roof or an entablature. In the Gothic style, arcades were often used as a decorative feature.
- Nave: The nave was the central part of a Christian church. It extends from the entrance to the aisle in front of the sanctuary. The nave is intended for the laypeople who are not supposed to enter the chancel, choir, and presbytery, which are reserved for the clergy. Gothic naves were divided into bays, which could hold images of saints or altars devoted to their worship. Bays also served as tombs for prominent church patrons. These naves were also lit by the clerestory, or a row of windows near the ceiling.
- Choir: The choir was positioned between the eastern end of the nave and the altar. It was the place for the singers who were part of the liturgy.

- Altar: In Christianity, the altar is the place where worshippers can partake in the Eucharist, a symbolic eating of the body and drinking of the blood of Christ. In Gothic cathedrals, the altar was the centerpiece, emphasized by the apse.

- Apse: An apse was a semicircular area behind the altar. It was ornately decorated with high-end materials like marble. Even the vault was sometimes decorated with mosaic designs.

- Ambulatory: The ambulatory is a passage that runs behind the apse and the altar, allowing pilgrims to circulate in the church without disturbing the congregation or the clergy.

- Narthex: The narthex is a covered vestibule at the western end of the church. It is separated from the nave by columns or a wall and includes an entryway to the nave. People who were not baptized were asked to remain in the narthex.

English Gothic

English Gothic architecture emerged as a distinctive style in three distinct phases. Early English Gothic (c. 1175–1265) corresponds to High Gothic in France. Common features include vaulting, quadripartite piers, and lancet-shaped windows. The Decorated period (c. 1250–1340) expanded traditional vault construction with extra ribs (called tiercerons and liernes). Window tracery, or thin lines of stonework that support large pieces of glass, was commonly carved into flowery shapes with intersecting, flowing lines.

The Perpendicular period (c. 1330–1540) introduced rectangular-shaped tracery and enormous vertical window panels. Pendant vaults look like upside-down triangles that appear to hang from the ceiling without structural support. They were gorgeous but tended to work better with smaller churches because they were not strong enough for huge high ceilings.

Gothic Windows

By the High Gothic period, architects were skilled at placing different kinds of windows and arches together on a single façade to create a visual impact. Sometimes different window types even appeared together under a single unifying arch. Here are a few popular gothic window features:

- Rose—This circular window, sometimes called the wheel window, was usually filled with ornate tracery. Often these were placed in or around the nave area.
- Lancet—The lancet arch is pointed. The windows under the pointed arch are typically long and narrow. They often appear as a series of windows alongside one another.
- Ogee—These curved arches come together in a point at the top. Each side is curved like an S to create a deep bend before the point.
- Trefoil—The trefoil pattern resembles leaves. Trefoil arches had three curved segments forming the arch but quatrefoil (four segments) and cinqfoil (five segments) were also popular.
- Perpendicular tracery—These long straight lines of tracery created a large, glass-paneled effect.

Canterbury Cathedral

Canterbury Cathedral was another famous cathedral that was destroyed by fire and then rebuilt in the Gothic style. It was a popular site for pilgrims because it housed the shrine of St. Thomas à Becket, archbishop of Canterbury, who was murdered by four of King Henry

II's knights inside the cathedral. Many miracles were witnessed near his tomb. After the 1174 fire, French architect William of Sens was hired to plan the cathedral's restoration, which included making major decisions about which sections should stay and which should be torn down. He decided the crypt should stay and the choir should go. All of these decisions required collaboration with the monks who lived there.

William of Sens had been working on the project for five years when he fell off scaffolding and hurt himself so badly that he had to return to France. An architect named William the Englishman took over the project. The new layout included room in the ambulatory and aisles for the steady stream of pilgrims who flowed through the church to see Becket's tomb.

A new choir was built as a huge structure over the crypt. It was longer than the previous version and held up by more piers. The vaulting included sexpartite arched ribs that were held in place by a keystone. Within the cathedral could be found both round and pointed arches. Capitals on the piers were elaborately carved. Two additional shrines were added to lengthen the central plan: the Trinity and Corona chapels. This was a more complex plan than the traditional French Gothic cathedral.

The Canterbury Tales

At the end of the fourteenth century, the English poet Geoffrey Chaucer composed his masterpiece, *The Canterbury Tales*. It is a collection of stories told by pilgrims on their way to visit Becket's tomb. Along the way, they entertain themselves by storytelling. The prologue to the tales, describing the various members of the party, is a favorite both for its frank discussion of contemporary life during this time and for its celebration of the coming of spring.

Expanding High Gothic

Each region of Europe took on its own particular Gothic characteristics. For example, German Gothic features include the hall church layout (in which vaults are above the nave and the aisles are the same height as the nave); high windows that often had no colored glass and so let in brighter light; huge towers and spires; lacy stonework; and no clerestory windows.

Italian gothic made adjustments to account for Italian weather. Italy has bright skies, so it was not necessary to have enormous windows. The Italians also used cloister vaults that resembled domes—a design that required less buttressing. They decorated with marble veneer, using fewer columns, which were spaced farther apart, and simple adornments.

THE EARLY RENAISSANCE

A New Humanism

The fourteenth century was marked by a renewed interest in the arts and sciences, especially in Italy. The Italians began reading and studying work by the Greeks and Romans with a new intensity. People were fascinated with Roman texts from the past and searched for as many surviving texts as they could find. Artists and scholars began to move away from the religious focus that had been at the heart of the culture of the Middle Ages. Instead they started thinking more about humans' feelings and experiences. They also studied the human body, and in art began depicting it more realistically. They even went so far as to question the Catholic Church, which had grown into a massive and often corrupt organization.

In 1453, disaster struck when Constantinople was conquered by the Ottoman Turks, marking the end of the Byzantine Empire. That empire had been a major presence in the East for a thousand years; now Constantinople became the Muslim city of Istanbul. Refugees from the sacked empire flooded into western Europe.

The Byzantine Empire had been formed from the eastern half of the old Roman Empire. Its common language was Greek, and its scholars studied Greek texts. The Byzantine refugees brought these books back to Italy and taught their welcoming countrymen about classical Greece.

Criticizing the Middle Ages

People in the early Renaissance tended to be critical of much medieval scholarship, which they felt had grown stale and dogmatic. They saw themselves standing at a bright point of knowledge, as if on a mountain. In the distance they could see another mountain: the age of classical Greece and Rome. In between, they beheld nothing but a long, dark middle age. Hence the name "Middle Ages" to refer to the period from the fall of Rome to the Renaissance, or "rebirth."

In the Middle Ages, architecture had been of supreme importance because it created great cathedrals and churches, the focus of much of society. In those days, painting and sculpture were thought of as means to decorate the cathedrals and churches. In the Renaissance, painting and sculpture achieved an importance apart from architecture.

As the arts changed, so did religion. The religious movement called the Reformation was spearheaded by a group of Protestant reformers who rejected the pope as an authority and began setting up their own churches, mostly in northern Europe. This effectively divided the Christian world into two parts.

Italy as the Center of the Renaissance

Italy was the center of the Renaissance in the intellectual and artistic sense, so much so that we sometimes refer to the Italian Renaissance. It was also the financial hub of the movement. Families such as Florence's Medici were wealthy patrons of painting, sculpture, and architecture. Trade was robust because of Italy's location between western Europe and the East. Merchants sold and exported luxury goods and textiles. Now people were wealthy because they were making money from commerce, not just land. These people sought to display their status by promoting initiatives in the arts and letters.

Pythagoras

Renaissance-era architects were particularly taken with Pythagoras, a Greek philosopher and mathematician. Although none of his works survive, he was often quoted by other Greek authors.

Filippo Brunelleschi

Filippo Brunelleschi (1377–1446), a sculptor, moved to Rome for several years to study ancient buildings and monuments. While there, he studied classical texts concerning the various architectural styles and the ratios on which they were based. He preferred the round classical columns to the pointy Gothic piers.

Upon returning to Florence, Brunelleschi was drafted into the effort to construct a dome for the rebuilt Florentine cathedral. The city's rulers wished to make the cathedral bigger and add a dome over its central octagonal section. This meant the dome would have to stretch 138 feet. The octagonal dome posed many problems, not least its size. It was not simple to build a hemispherical dome like that of the Pantheon; constructing an octagonal one was even more challenging. The dome needed to cover the cathedral would be too heavy to support itself, and the area was too wide for wooden centering to work.

Instead of using buttresses for support, Brunelleschi planned a system of stone ribs that stretched vertically from the bottom of the dome to the apex. These ribs were visible on the exterior of the structure and they eliminated the need for any centering to support the dome. For each of these main exterior ribs, there were two secondary ribs tucked away and not visible from the outside. Then he built two thin, horizontal shells that were placed together as a single dome, an innovation that allowed him to build the biggest dome anyone had ever seen. The walls of the dome were very steep, which reduced the outward thrust. The dome, as a result, looks a bit pointed compared to the more hemispherical domes we have examined. It remains a dominant fixture on the Florence skyline even today.

Leon Battista Alberti

Leon Battista Alberti (1404–1472) was less a technical architect than an architectural theorist. He was an important thinker of his day, having come from an academic Florentine family who had been exiled. After his studies, he became the chancellor's secretary in Rome. Here he studied the ancient works of art and met many artists. He used classical theory and architecture to make statements about society and the way it was ordered. Aside from architecture, he was also a student of physics and the natural sciences and he applied both to his building plans.

Alberti was inspired to pursue architecture when he read Vitruvius's *Ten Books on Architecture*. Renaissance architects respected his work greatly, as an important source of information about classical Rome. Alberti subscribed to Vitruvius's ideas about proportional systems, like finding a central area through use of a circle, hexagon, or square area. He believed that churches should be part of the cityscape. In order for this to happen they needed to be visible on all sides and placed at a higher elevation.

He thought about private house plans too. For example, guestrooms should be near the entrance so guests could be comfortable and have freedom to come and go as they pleased. Parents' and children's rooms should be close together. Bedrooms are best positioned toward the rising sun, to awake the inhabitants in the morning.

Kitchens should be set off but close to the dining room. He thought a lot about convenience for inhabitants, and hygiene as well—a surprisingly modern concern.

He also believed that manufacturing operations with waste and noxious gases should be distanced from the residential part of a city. One of the first to think about urban planning, he believed a house in an urban setting should have less ornamentation so that it fits in with all the other buildings on the block. A country house could be as decorative as it wanted. He set parameters about the types and quality of building materials, such as sand, timber, and lime—for example, timber should be clean and without knots.

THE HIGH RENAISSANCE
Great Achievements

Most of the accomplishments we most closely associate with the Renaissance occurred during the late fifteenth century and early sixteenth century, a period known as the High Renaissance. Among the artists working during this time were Leonardo da Vinci, Michelangelo, and Raphael. These years were also turbulent politically; there were invasions and takeovers and shifting borders throughout the Italian peninsula. Toward the end of the century, a religious fanatic named Girolamo Savonarola took power in Florence and condemned the arts as "vanities." Although he was eventually overthrown, Florence faded as the artistic hub of the movement; Rome was now the creative center of Italy.

The Central Plan

Leonardo da Vinci (1452–1519) was in many respects a successor to Alberti. He was a polymath with gifts in painting, sculpture, architecture, science, and humanism. For a long time people had spoken of the circle as a divine shape, a symbol of symmetry and harmony. Alberti had written about the presence of the circle in nature and had pointed out that ancient temples had often been circular in plan. Vitruvius also said that if a man fanned out his arms and legs as if he were standing in the middle of a circle, his navel would be positioned right in the center. Leonardo illustrated this concept in his famous anatomical drawing *Vitruvian Man* (c. 1490).

When Leonardo developed plans for churches, he used this ideal of the circle as an organizing principle. Leonardo's drawings for churches—none of which were built—show them with domes. Donato Bramante (1444–1514) put this plan into effect. He designed the Tempietto (1502), a domed commemorative tomb, in Rome. King Ferdinand and Queen Isabella of Spain (Christopher Columbus's benefactors) commissioned the monument in the spot where St. Peter was believed to have been martyred. Bramante planned a circular temple, built in the Doric order with sixteen columns, a frieze, and a balustrade. A hemispherical dome tops the building. Bramante selected the Doric order as a nod to Vitruvius's belief that a temple's order should reflect the god whom the temple was built to honor, in this case an active male god. Bramante treated the building as one big room. It was a small space that could not hold many people at once and was probably meant to be admired from the outside. This is reinforced by the fact that the door is in an awkward position opposite the altar.

The Dome

Domes, a majestic part of Byzantine buildings, experienced a resurgence during the Renaissance. Usually the dome appeared over the central space of a building. Here they might be combined with a classical temple front, much as Hadrian had done with the Pantheon in Rome. Byzantine buildings often had trussed domes. Roman domes were often made of a single concrete or brick shell. In the Renaissance, builders began using the double-shell, as Brunelleschi had done in Florence; this allowed them to create enormous domes that would be stable.

Features of Renaissance Domes

- Saucer dome: A bit flat in presentation so that it does not look quite like a hemisphere, reminiscent of a saucer that has been turned upside down.
- Hemispherical dome: A perfect hemisphere. The shape lends itself to being built very tall. Usually boasts a cupola.
- Oval dome: Appears over an oval section of the church such as the nave.
- Triple-shelled dome: The external dome is held in place by hidden supports like a brick cone. This support system can then be covered up by another smaller dome that is placed on top.

St. Peter's Basilica in Rome

By the time of the Renaissance, St. Peter's church in Rome, the spiritual center of Christendom, was more than a thousand years old, decaying and decrepit. Pope Julius II commissioned Michelangelo to create a tomb for him that would be placed in the basilica. Both men soon realized that the enormous monument would never fit into the old church, so the pope hired Bramante to help him decide what kinds of additions needed to be made to the old structure. They worked through possibilities for an extension before deciding to rebuild the church entirely.

Given the scope of the plan, it's not surprising that realizing it took a very long time. Bramante developed a Greek-cross plan and decided to install an enormous dome that would secure the basilica's place in Roman history. He did not plan it very well though, and the piers in his plan were not strong enough to support the heavy dome. Bramante died before they had made any real progress and the project sat. Fifty years later, Pope Paul III had cultivated a building fund to resume the project, and commissioned Michelangelo. He was primarily a sculptor but took on the project as an opportunity to please God, and signed on for a small fee.

Michelangelo realized that the dome as it was originally conceived would not work. He changed the plans so that the dome would be hemispherical, and added more stone ribs to the outside of the dome—increasing the number from eight to sixteen. We know now that this would not have worked either because the thrust of the ribs would have been too much for the drum of the dome, which might have crumbled. Michelangelo died before he was able to build the dome.

The dome's construction was now taken over by Giacomo della Porta (c. 1533–1602). He increased its height and added a cupola. He used columns and varied the entablature so that instead of running straight across in one single piece, it was interrupted at the base, protruding with each set of double columns. This is known as a broken entablature and here it buttresses the dome and forces the outward thrust onto the piers and arches below. The entire project was finished in the seventeenth century, with significant additions to the interior of the church by the sculptor Gianlorenzo Bernini (1598–1680).

Mannerism

Scholars often correlate Raphael's death in 1520 with the end of the Renaissance. When it ended, new artistic movements rose in its place. One style that emerged at the end of the Renaissance was Mannerism (from the Italian word *maiera*, meaning "style" or "stylishness"). Some have criticized the movement as a reaction against the symmetry and harmony of the High Renaissance, but it was inspired by the possibilities that High Renaissance figures had opened for younger artists.

Renaissance artists had studied and observed nature but Mannerists drew their inspiration and models from other works of art. They most frequently illustrated the human body in exaggerated, twisting, provocative positions and unlikely situations. The movement was not concerned with balance and symmetry; the paintings seemed crowded and unstable. The Mannerists also rejected the proportions that were so crucial to Renaissance art. Sometimes it was even difficult to understand the narrative that was being expressed in the art. It seemed geared toward a tight-knit group of elite intellectuals, and perhaps no one else was really expected to understand it.

Although it was expressed primarily in painting and sculpture, Mannerism was also occasionally manifested in architecture, for example in the Villa Farnese in Caprarola. The building eschews the kind of ornamentation characteristic of the High Renaissance and instead relies on clean, spare lines for its visual impact.

Artists in Society

Some of the elite nature of Mannerism was due to the fact that the artists themselves were enjoying a new place in society. After the Renaissance, they were considered among the scholars and humanists whereas previously painters, sculptors, and architects had mostly been considered nothing more than craftsmen.

ANDREA PALLADIO

Artistic Discipline

Andrea Palladio (1508–1580) was one of the most influential architects of all time and he is, in fact, widely regarded as the first modern architect. This is because he was the first person to work on architecture as a full-time job without any side projects. All the other Renaissance figures worked in many disciplines at once (Leonardo was notorious for starting projects and taking years to finish them). From Palladio forward, being an architect was considered a job.

Palladio was trained as a stone mason in Padua. His work caught the attention of a wealthy benefactor, Gian Giorgio Trissino, who was an intellectual. Trissino wanted to provide Palladio with a true humanist education so he sent him to Rome where he could study the ancient monuments and read classical architectural texts such as those by Vitruvius and modern works by people such as Alberti.

In Rome, Palladio was especially taken with the proportions used by ancient builders. These proportions would have a powerful impact on all his work. He built all kinds of structures, from churches and civil buildings to farmhouses. He was preoccupied by the idea of creating a tranquil country retreat away from urban life, a notion that was an important ideal in the Renaissance. Most of his country houses were built in an area north of Venice called the Veneto. These homes were working farms that were usually owned and run by Venetian nobles' sons.

Palladio's *Four Books of Architecture*

Palladio's *Four Books of Architecture* were illustrated treatises on architecture as a formal practice and discipline. In these books he explored a range of topics from the classical orders to city planning and temple building. He discussed the principles of building arches, bridges, and baths in Roman building. As well, from ancient writings he tried to envision what Roman domestic architecture might have looked like.

Proportions in Architecture

Palladio is considered to be Alberti's successor in architecture. Alberti had said that certain proportions can make things we see or hear especially pleasing for our minds, a concept that fascinated Palladio. As a result, his plans always included whole-number ratios. He then organized these into a firm system of proportions that would invoke a sense of harmony in architecture. He emphasized convenience and practicality in his buildings, but he also thought it was important that architecture please and delight. This component of his work influenced other countries for centuries.

Music as a Format for Architecture

Innovators such as Palladio were taken with the way music is organized. Music notes need to blend together in intervals and ratios to sound nice. If you stray from these intervals, the music sounds discordant. So the idea was that music notes sound good together if they respect a certain relationship or ratio. Palladio believed that using harmonic proportions in architecture would make it look as good as music sounds.

Vicenza Basilica

Most of Palladio's buildings are located in and around Vicenza. Even though he was rooted in classicism, he often used humble materials that were not overly luxurious. To achieve symmetry, he often designed groups of rooms around a central hall.

In 1549 he remodeled the Vicenza basilica. He turned what had been a medieval town hall into a two-story building with arcading. He designed exterior arches that were supported with large columns and then included smaller columns on the inside of the big ones. The lintel above the columns was flat but the large middle space between the columns was arched. The opening was therefore divided into three parts, the main portal and the two narrow entries flanked by the columns that appeared on either side of it. He used this pattern on many of his designs. It was hugely popular and became known as the Palladian motif. It was copied everywhere.

The windows on his basilica had tripartite openings. Today, the typical Palladian window consists of two square openings with a long arched window in the middle.

Teatro Olimpico

The Teatro Olimpico (1580) in Vicenza was modeled after a classical Greek or Roman theater. Seats were tiered and situated in a horseshoe. One of the most influential things Palladio planned was a permanent background to the stage with a scene depicted on it. The scene was an urban piazza with a few streets in view and a false perspective that created a three-dimensional effect. This quickly became the prototype for theaters and opera houses and is still used today. The interior ceiling of the Teatro Olimpico is painted to look like the sky.

Villa Barbaro

The Villa Barbaro at Maser (1555–1559) was a country home that functioned as a gentleman's farm. It had an asymmetrical master plan. End pavilions sat on either side of the main living block. These pavilions were connected to the main part of the house by arcades. The building was slightly elevated so that it was possible to admire the landscape from the windows. Palladio made room for all the farm equipment and supplies in one structure. This included a place to store equipment, hay, and other supplies needed by the livestock. There was also a spot for threshing grain.

The rooms in the villa are delightful, filled with light and decorated with colorful frescoes. The walls are topped with barrel-vaulted ceilings. There are classical features such as columns and pediments and even a balcony in one room.

The exterior of the villa was that of a structure that was an important public building, even though it was a private residence. Palladio used a column and pediment, features that had previously been used only for temples. The style had great influence, and it is used for homes even today. Scholars think that his innovations with the columned entrance may have been a product of his confusion about what Vitruvius was talking about when he discussed the history of the megaron. Palladio didn't know what a megaron was so he may have interpreted the work as saying Greek houses looked like Greek temples.

Palladio's Influence on British Architecture

Later British designers were especially influenced by Palladio's work and writings. They were taken with the way he juxtaposed his descriptions of his own work with Roman buildings that were already established. They were also impressed with his use of columns and pediments as well as sea scallops and masks. In the 1700s, British builders used these sensibilities to develop a classical British style. They created a variation on Palladio's style by adding rich decoration to their exteriors.

Palladio's Influence on American Architecture

Since Palladio's work appeared overseas, most Americans never saw it. They were, however, able to read his books. These made a major impact in part because the drawings were so clear and easy to understand, unlike anything that had been published before.

He also described the orders and their respective entablatures in great detail. His portico, especially the pedimented and two-tiered variations, was a favorite element in many American buildings. It had been used for ancient temples but it started to appear on plantation houses and stately buildings, including public buildings in Washington such as the Supreme Court. Five-section houses became very popular in Maryland and Virginia. These homes often had a two-story center with one-story wings. Jefferson loved Palladio's work and publicly praised it. As well, he employed some of Palladio's principles in his construction of Monticello.

PRE-COLUMBIAN AMERICA

Complex Civilizations in the New World

The term *pre-Columbian* refers to the people and civilizations that existed in the Americas before the Europeans arrived in 1492. Some of these societies were highly developed with networks of city-states, road systems, and efficient building traditions. Their achievements are especially powerful when you consider the physiography of the region. There were chilly mountains, tropical forests, desert valleys, and coastlines, adding up to a complex of ecological systems. Despite the diversity in terrain and resources, the pre-Columbian Americans developed advanced building methods. The Inca used such methods and city-planning techniques; indeed, they have been compared to the Romans.

The Inca

The city of Cuzco, founded in 1430 in what is today Peru, was the center of the Inca civilization. The great ruler Pachacuti and his son organized the city-state and then set to conquering neighboring territories until they had amassed an empire triple the size it had been when they came to power. By the 1480s, the Inca Empire was so enormous that it stretched across the entire western coast of South America.

The Inca Empire centered on the Andes Mountains and spread out over large sections of what are now Ecuador, Bolivia, Chile, and Columbia. Under such a large empire, there was tremendous diversity in the landscape, and the Inca were masterminds at using every bit of it. Farmers carved terraced fields into the steep mountainsides where they planted root vegetables that thrived in cold weather. They developed pastures on the mountain peaks for llamas, which were used for traveling and carrying communications. Capitalizing on the fertility of the valleys, they nestled maize and bean fields between the mountain ranges. They planted warm-weather crops such as squash, tomatoes, and fruit in the tropical climates situated farther inland. The people on the sandy coasts fished and hunted.

Most of the town and city centers were found in the valleys. The empire emphasized a strict hierarchy under the emperor, who was called the Sapa Inca. This supreme ruler was more than just a king; he was the "son of the sun." He made frequent trips to survey his empire and to double-check his subjects' loyalty. When the Sapa Inca appeared, everyone was expected to show their humility by taking off their shoes and loading up their backs with a bundle or something that was a burden to carry.

The nobles were the next most important people in the Incan hierarchy. This class included the emperor's children, priests, judges, and army officers. The farmers, laborers, and craftsman came after them. This class worked very hard and established tight-knit communities that came together to share in domestic tasks. These groups, called *ayllus*, were like families.

Inca Gods

Temples were built for worshiping a number of deities of which the creator, Viracocha, was considered to be the most important. Inti was the sun god who was honored as the father of the Sapa Inca. Inti was married to his sister Mama Quilla (or Mama Killa), the moon. Pachamama was the goddess of earth, while Illapa, the weather god, ruled thunder, lighting, and rainstorms. There was a temple to Inti in the middle of every city. To honor the gods, sacrifice was a major part of their worship rituals. Incan temples, although attractive, were simple and tended to look very similar to one another. They were built of stone blocks that were laid without mortar. Each had a rectangular shape and a wooden or thatch roof.

Machu Picchu

Machu Picchu is the most famous site of Incan ruins, not least because it is one of the only locations found relatively intact. Since it was hardly the policy of the Spanish conquerors of the Inca to leave buildings intact, the chances are that in the case of Machu Picchu they probably never saw it. A popular hiking site today for visitors to the Inca Trail, it is at an elevation of more than 7,700 feet in the Andes Mountains, about fifty miles northwest of Cuzco. It was laid out like a large palace complex and archaeologists believe it was used as a getaway for the elite. From the ruins we can see that there was room for about 1,000 people to live in very close quarters. These people likely would have included kings, priests, and temple virgins.

The grandest buildings like palaces and temples were built at the very top of the site. The buildings were made of white granite and stone. The Princess's Palace was two levels of beautifully carved stone. One temple, called the Temple of the Three Windows, is a

The Pyramid of Khufu is the main structure in the complex of pyramids at Giza in Egypt. It was completed about 2560 B.C.E.

Machu Picchu (fifteenth century), a relatively intact Incan site, was undiscovered by the Spanish due to its soaring location more than 7,000 feet into the sky in the Andes Mountains.

The city of Pompeii, buried by a volcanic eruption in C.E. 79, has been excavated by modern archaeologists.

The end columns at the Parthenon (447 B.C.E.–432 B.C.E.) are positioned slightly closer together than those in the middle, which makes the composition livelier.

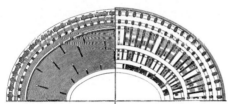

The Coliseum (C.E. 72–80) included enough seats for 50,000 spectators. It was designed as a continuously rising tier.

The Great Wall of China (third century B.C.E.– C.E. seventeenth century) is the most extraordinary fortification in the world. It includes four great walls that were built to protect China from the Mongols.

Saint Basil's Cathedral in Moscow (1555–1561) was built with nine separate chapels and eight domes.

The seventeenth-century Taj Mahal, in the Indian city of Agra, was built as a tomb for the wife of a Mughal emperor.

The Leaning Tower of Pisa (1173–1372) includes six stories of repeating arcaded galleries. The foundation on the building site was soft, which is why the tower leans.

Trinity Church (1872–1877) in Boston was built in eclectic style. The main plan is based on a Latin-cross basilica.

The roof of the Wainwright Building (1891) in St. Louis, Missouri, was capped with a heavy cornice. A decorated frieze sat just below it, punctured with the occasional bull's-eye window.

At more than 2,700 feet, Burj Khalifa (2004–2010) in the United Arab Emirates is the tallest man-made structure in the world.

The Chrysler Building (1928–1930) in New York City was designed with Art Deco style, including stainless steel and geometric patterns.

Fallingwater (1936–1939) was built by Frank Lloyd Wright with three horizontal terraces positioned over a natural waterfall.

The Guggenheim Bilbao (1997) in Spain was designed with a mix of intertwined glass, titanium, and limestone.

thirty-five-foot-long, forty-five-foot-wide hall with three windows made in a trapezoid shape.

Thousands of steps lead to plazas and residential areas and a cemetery, while the main entrance leads directly to the Inca Trail. Scholars believe the Inca Trail, which is more than twenty-five miles long, was built especially for Machu Picchu and that its purpose was to give visitors a chance to prepare for the holy experience that awaited them. The trail takes about four days to hike. Stepped agricultural terraces appear on the eastern and western sides. It certainly was not easy to get water up to that elevation, so the settlement was probably watered by an aqueduct system. One of the most revered monuments is a large carved stone that functioned as a sundial. Called Intihuatana, it was known as the "post where the sun is tied."

Incan Roads

The road system in the Inca Empire was one of the most impressive in the ancient world. There were some 25,000 miles of road, many of which were paved with stone. These bridges and roads were often only wide enough for two llamas to pass one another. Two main highways ran parallel, one along the coast and the other through the highlands. These roads were always packed with travelers. The large number of river gorges complicated road building. To span these cliffs, the Incas made bridges from braided reeds that could be anchored to either side by a stone platform. An inspector came by regularly to examine them for safety and make any necessary repairs.

Inca Homes

Most ordinary Inca homes were made of mud bricks, stone, or adobe. They were simple structures with a single stove to heat the interior, and a thatched grass roof. There was typically just one entrance covered with a cloth and perhaps a small, high window. The clay stove warmed the structure in the cold weather but there were no chimneys, so the smoke escaped through the window or the roof. Furnishings were modest—there might be a stone bench, niches for storage, and stone pegs for hanging things. Throughout the city, cold spring water ran through a stone channel for washing.

Administrative buildings were often built with shaped granite blocks that were placed together without mortar. This was a smart innovation since it increased the chances that if a building were to be shaken by an earthquake, the bricks would fall neatly back into place. The builders shaped the blocks by hand with small hammers and bronze chisels.

Aztecs

The Aztecs lived in the Valley of Mexico in the thirteenth century. The remains of their capital, Tenochtitlán, lie under what is now Mexico City. At its height, the Aztec Empire stretched from what is now northern Mexico to Guatemala and El Salvador.

Tenochtitlán was originally a series of islands but the Aztecs used earth to fill in the spaces between them. The city was organized as a grid and was divided into four sections that were bounded by four long roads. Right in the center of these sections was a huge plaza that was used for social gatherings at the ball courts, cultural and religious rituals, and worship at the pyramids and temples. The main thoroughfare was the widest road that ran through the center of the city, called Avenue of the Dead.

The Aztecs had many rituals, including human sacrifice, and, lest anyone forget, the center of the square boasted a gruesome rack of skulls. The center of religious life was the pyramid which held shrines to the gods, temples, and areas for human sacrifice. Their religious practices included pulling hearts out of victims so that they could offer them, still pumping, to the gods. The Aztecs built the Pyramid of the Sun and the Pyramid of the Moon with mud bricks and limestone. Towering over 200 feet into the sky and 730 feet long on each side of the base, the Pyramid of the Sun was one of the largest structures ever built in the pre-Columbian Americas. Built in the center of the city along the Avenue of the Dead, it dominated the landscape in Tenochtitlàn. Religious symbolism heavily influenced Aztec construction and the way buildings were positioned in the city plan. The pyramid shape was meant to represent a sacred mountain. The Pyramid of the Sun was built on top of a long underground cave which was believed to be the place where the gods created worlds. The Pyramid of the Moon, built at the northern end of the Avenue of the Dead, is smaller at just over one hundred and fifty feet tall. It was built in stages as seven different pyramids stacked on top of one another.

Mayans

We know a lot about the Mayans because they developed a hyper-organized system of writing and recording history. The Mayan civilization was located in what is now Guatemala. This region included the most cities and independent states of all the pre-Columbian civilizations. Tikal was the most impressive of all of them with a population of 60,000.

Tikal centered on a large open space called the Great Plaza. The most important buildings and monuments were positioned around this public area. The North Acropolis of Tikal is a group of pyramids that are densely packed together at the north end of the Great Plaza. At this site there are also inscribed steles, which are memorial slabs that stick out of the ground. Stone palaces and temples dominated the busy center of the city. The homes outside of the city were modest both in size and material. These small structures were usually made of wood and thatch and packed in closely to one another.

When the Spaniards began their voyages of conquest to Latin America at the end of the sixteenth century, they conquered pre-Columbian America very quickly. The indigenous cultures and their methods of building vanished and were replaced by Europeans.

BAROQUE STYLE

The Power of the Dramatic

Baroque is characterized by a sense of dramatic emotion and energy. The movement began in Rome after the Renaissance, partly as a reaction against the Protestant Reformation. At that time, the Catholic Church commissioned a great deal of art and architecture. Although the church was wealthy and powerful, reformers such as Martin Luther and John Calvin questioned its ethical and theological foundations. Donations from wealthy church members were misused by the church leaders who lined their pockets and led worldly lives (Pope Alexander VI, for example, had nine children while he held office, including Lucrezia Borgia and her brother Cesare).

The church raised additional funds by selling pardons and indulgences, often at exorbitant prices. More importantly to reformers, such a practice implied that the church had the power to remit sins, rather than God. This intense corruption ignited a German monk named Martin Luther, and in 1517 he nailed a document to the door of the All Saints' Church in Wittenberg, Germany. The document contained ninety-five "theses" or propositions about the Catholic Church, none of which the pope and Catholic hierarchy could accept.

The Catholic Church was helpless against the growing number of dissenters. They realized they could no longer single out naysayers and make public examples of them by declaring them heretics and punishing them. They were suffering from a public image problem and they needed to do some positive, civic-minded things to change it. The Catholic Counter-Reformation was their program to reform themselves and encourage people to come back to the church.

The Council of Trent

The Council of Trent, which met between 1545 and 1563, was the centerpiece of the Catholic Counter-Reformation. The council was made up of bishops and theologians. The goal was to restore peace among Christians through reaffirming the morals and ethics of the church leaders and defining the doctrine that was shared with followers. Through their theories and policies, the council encouraged the Baroque building boom.

The Dramatization of Art

The Baroque style reinforced the Catholic beliefs but in a violently theatrical way. Baroque architecture emphasized the contrast between dark and light, called chiaroscuro, to add drama to all its forms. Baroque buildings, by using curved lines, concaves, and oval shapes, played optical tricks that brought out textures and complexities. Ceilings were painted, walls were gilded. Often spectators felt as if they were in motion. Sculpture, painting, and architecture were sensual.

Features of Baroque

- Lavish, dramatic paintings featured on ceilings and walls, often containing optical illusions
- Spiraled columns
- Grand, sweeping stairways that emphasized grandeur and space
- Domes
- Long, curvilinear forms
- Complicated shapes

Gianlorenzo Bernini

The Basilica of St. Peter in Rome has incredible meaning and importance for the Christian religion and is considered to be the center of the Catholic faith. Pilgrims come from all over the world to visit the structure. When Sixtus V came to the papacy the planned rebuilding of it had again stalled. Michelangelo had been working on the dome but when he died construction halted. Pope Sixtus V decided to resume the building and to redesign the piazza in front of it, which included a forty-foot Egyptian obelisk. After Pope Sixtus V died, several other architects worked on the project before the dome was finally consecrated in 1626. In 1629, Gianlorenzo Bernini (1598–1680), a prodigy in sculpture, architecture, and city planning, was asked to serve as the official architect, a position he held until his death.

Bernini's work dominated the Baroque movement in Rome for years. The interior of St. Peter's is the best example of his influence. One of the most marvelous sites to see today is his nearly ninety-foot-high bronze baldacchino, the permanent canopy in the middle of the nave that sits over the supposed site of Peter's tomb.

The Bronze for the Baldacchino

Bernini completed the baldacchino during the papacy of Urban VIII, a member of the powerful Barberini family. Because of the amount of bronze needed for the structure, Bernini appealed for assistance to the pope, who ordered the bronze stripped from the roof of the Pantheon. Thus the saying sprang up, "What the *barbari* (barbarians) could not do has been done by the Barberini."

Bernini designed St. Peter's Square, an open space recognized all over the world. It is where the faithful assemble to hear the pope deliver his blessings. It includes an oval section, in the center of which is positioned the Vatican obelisk, and a trapezoidal section at the entrance of the church. Bernini surrounded the piazza with 284 columns and crowned them with statues of saints. The colonnades stretch out like two great arms, welcoming the pilgrims who come to pay their respects to St. Peter's tomb. The piazza is big enough to accommodate more than 250,000 people.

Bernini also designed the Scala Regia, a ceremonial staircase, for Pope Alexander VII. The stairs get narrower as they get higher, which creates the illusion that they go on forever. There is a landing halfway up the passage, lit from a hidden source. This creates a dramatic and thought-provoking effect.

Cultural Distinctions

As the Baroque spread throughout Europe it adapted to regional styles. In general, in northern Europe the Baroque style was less flamboyant and openly theatrical than in the south. The English especially were more restrained. In Spain and Latin America, the buildings were recognizable by their intense sculptures, while French Baroque was comparatively reserved. The French favored a rectilinear approach with predictable geometry instead of the curves and convex shapes that were so popular in Italy. The style in France was in line with the strict political system that evolved under Louis XIV.

The Louvre

Louis XIV maintained strict control over all parts of his kingdom, and the building and crafts guilds, for that reason, were under his control. He established an academy that conveyed a national style pointing to the absolute glory of France. The Louvre, then a palace, was rebuilt. Bernini actually submitted a proposal for the project but it was rejected because it did not look French enough; his main idea was to add a curved wall.

The three men who took on the project, painter Charles Lebrun, architect Louis Le Vau, and physician Claude Perrault, developed something more restrained with a classical symmetry. They set the style for seventeenth-century French architecture.

Each window in the Louvre is topped by a small pediment. The windows are separated by pairs of columns that stretch two stories high. These columns are linked by an entablature that stretches continuously around the building. The roof is encircled by a balustrade, or railing supported by rungs, which accentuates the length of the structure. The central pavilion is designed like the front of a Roman temple with a pediment.

SIR CHRISTOPHER WREN

Rebuilding London

Sir Christopher Wren (1632–1723) was one of England's most distinguished architects during the seventeenth century. He was educated at Westminster School and then attended Oxford University. He was a novice inventor, with particular gifts in math and astronomy. Among other things, he invented a machine that would allow someone to write in the dark, and a transparent beehive so that people could observe the bees at work. He was appointed professor of astronomy at Oxford University before his interest in physics and engineering drew him into architecture. He was commissioned to design a theater in Oxford and a chapel in Cambridge. Then he took a trip to Paris where he saw the Baroque style. Both the French and the Italian versions of Baroque inspired him greatly.

The Royal Society

Wren was one of the founders of an elite group of English thinkers, an organization that still flourishes today. The Royal Society was founded by a group of natural philosophers in 1660 under the patronage of King Charles II. Today it sponsors scientific conferences and provides opportunities for academic discussion.

The Great Fire of London

In 1666 fire destroyed most of the city of London. The fire had started in a baker's house near London Bridge. It spread quickly to other sections of town where it engulfed warehouses full of flammable materials. London at that time was still very much a medieval city with narrow lanes and wooden houses. Winds easily carried the inferno down the city streets of tightly packed houses with tar roofs.

The fire burned for several days. Before it was extinguished it had destroyed 13,000 homes, almost ninety churches, and a number of city landmarks, including St. Paul's Cathedral. Christopher Wren was brought on to redesign the whole city. His projects included more than fifty churches, royal commissions, universities, and the cathedral. His first set of plans was too revolutionary for the people of London and he had to scrap them. They wanted to stick to the tradition of English cathedrals. He toned down the designs a little bit and was appointed Surveyor of the Royal Works in 1669, which meant that all government building in the country came under his authority. He was knighted in 1673.

Wren's English Baroque

Christopher Wren became one of the main exponents of the Baroque style in England, but his version of the Baroque was quite different from that found in southern Europe. In England it was more restrained, Protestant, and more obviously linked to classical sensibilities.

Wren frequently commissioned interior decorations from Grinling Gibbons (1648–1721), a wood carver who produced elegant carvings of items from nature such as flowers, small animals, and cherubs. Gibbons worked on the choir to include the choir screen carved from limewood (also called linden or basswood).

St. Paul's Cathedral

The old St. Paul's in London had been a Gothic building with a Latin-cross plan. Wren originally wanted to change the plan to a centralized structure with a Greek cross but that idea was rejected.

Protestant church leaders insisted on a longitudinal plan with a lengthy nave. He eventually resubmitted his proposal, which was technically a nave-and-aisle layout, but just barely. In his new plan, the nave was only slightly longer than the choir, which made it very close to his original central plan.

The final design for the cathedral blended several inspirations including the Louvre, buildings in Renaissance Italy, the classical orders, and the early Christian basilica. The dome is 300 feet high and 112 feet in diameter, second only to St. Peter's in Rome. It was built to be a dominant feature on the London skyline, and even today amid the welter of skyscrapers it stands out. The dome is a system of domes built atop one another. The main dome, made of timber and lead, and the stone lantern above it rests on a brick cone that is hidden inside the structure. This cone is resting on a smaller interior dome. The dome is ringed on the inside with a walkway so that visitors can peer down at the floor far below. The best view of the interior dome is from the nave itself.

Two towers are decidedly Baroque in their execution here. They flank the main section of the building and have curved walls just under the spires and pediments over the windows of the second story and round arches over the windows on the main level. The façade between the towers is two stories with pairs of Corinthian columns. The second-story columns support a decorated pediment, and each level of columns also supports an entablature.

The structure is comprised of saucer domes over the choir, nave, and aisle. These saucer domes were decorated with elaborate mosaics.

Inigo Jones

We should take a moment to mention Inigo Jones because he is frequently overshadowed by his contemporary, Christopher Wren.

Jones was the first notable architect in England but he, like many men during his time, dabbled in so many things that he receives less attention than he deserves for his building designs.

Jones was the first Englishman to bring the classicism of the Italian Renaissance to Britain. He introduced the proportions so critical to Roman building and was mesmerized by Andrea Palladio's theories and designs. He worked as the Surveyor of the King's Works under James I and built the Queen's House in Greenwich with unmistakable Palladian style. Before his influence, these types of buildings had been developed in what was called a Tudor style (after an earlier royal dynasty). Jones also introduced the use of the truss as a roof. In these innovative structures, a central post was supported by rafters. A larger roof was then built over it. Christopher Wren achieved a similar innovation when he built the dome at St Paul's.

It was not just Jones's exteriors that made an impact; he designed interiors with tall columns, windows, and ceiling frescoes, and the very first self-supported spiral staircase that had ever been built in England.

His Work Is His Memorial

Wren's gravestone at St. Paul's Cathedral is etched with a Latin inscription that translates as, "If you seek his memorial, look about you."

ROCOCO

Light, Bright Luxury

Rococo flourished in eighteenth-century Europe from about 1700–1775. There is still some dispute about whether Rococo is its own independent style or simply a modification of Baroque. As an art form, it was witty and fantastical in its expression with lovers and cupids at picnics and gods and goddesses in romantic scenarios. Rococo was used for interior design in France, and the Neoclassically rooted architects there found it to be excessive as a building style. In truth, despite its whimsy, it was fairly dedicated to the classical orders. The images depicted in its art were also in the vein of Greek and Roman traditions. At times, Rococo architects were reacting against the strictness of Louis XIV's building rules and the resulting Baroque. They were trying to establish something more laid-back and personal. They brought in curves and natural motifs, scrolls, swags, mirrors, and gilded plaster. Ornament was all over everything including the windows, ceilings, walls, and doors.

What's in a Name?

The term *Rococo* comes from the French word *rocaille*, which refers to rockwork and shellwork, a motif that appeared frequently in Rococo designs.

Features of Rococo
- Often the main plan is asymmetrical
- Curvilinear forms that resemble the letters S and C
- A highly styled acanthus leaf

- Pastel colors
- Playful subjects

Distinguishing Between Baroque and Rococo

As we have said, Rococo is often considered to be a modification of the Baroque style just more . . . relaxed. However, there are some key differences to keep in mind when distinguishing between the two. Baroque was popular for important buildings such as cathedrals and royal palaces. Rococo translated well to the houses of the aristocracy. Rococo is usually lighter and brighter with gentle pastels in intimate settings. Baroque uses very bold, dark colors for massive structures.

Salons

One of those more intimate settings where Rococo was particularly appropriate was the Salon. The Salon was the stylish center of French society in the eighteenth century. These salons were typically run by smart, charming, and wealthy women, often in their forties or older. People came to share in conversations about art and culture, eat, and listen to music. Rococo style added a bright liveliness to these chatty rooms with lightly colored walls and glinting gilded relief patterns. Mirrors added to the airy feeling and playfulness by bouncing reflections all around the room. Cherubic cupids appeared on wall surfaces.

Chinoiserie

Chinoiserie was a decorative style inspired by Asia. European designers were taken with the exotic imports from China and Japan such as silk and porcelain. They attempted to create their own designs with Chinese figures, dragons, and pagodas. The word *chinoiserie* comes from *chinois*, the French word for Chinese.

The Enlightenment

The eighteenth century was known as the Age of Enlightenment. Intellectuals questioned society's close ties to the church and examined all matters with reason and intellect. This spirit inspired scientific investigation and a secular examination of everything from the way people and governments organize themselves to phenomena of nature. Figures such as the French philosopher Voltaire (1694–1778) questioned authority and broke from a strictly religious view of the world.

These attitudes churned up sentiments that eventually led to the French and American Revolutions. With such serious concerns, proponents of the Enlightenment tended to regard Rococo as frivolous. Rococo with its playful images and wit appeared as an optimistic countercurrent to the larger context.

The Residenz

Despite its condemnation by some thinkers, Rococo thrived throughout Europe as a decorative style. Some of the best examples of Rococo as an architectural style appear in Germany. German architect Balthasar Neumann designed an ornate building in Bavaria called the Residenz, or the Episcopal Palace (1720–1744) (the interior was completed in 1780). This building is an outstanding example of palace architecture. The counts of Schönborn, who lived in the house, were very wealthy and liked nice things. They envisioned a house full of splendor and used their money and connections to hire a team of artists to decorate the house. The leading architects of Germany were involved, as were the best sculptors and carvers. Giovanni Battista Tiepolo (1696–1770), the greatest fresco painter of the eighteenth century, painted the enormous ceiling fresco, said to be the largest in the world.

The main plan of the palace was similar to that of Versailles: very long with side wings and an open court at the entrance. The columns echoed the classical orders but the spaces in the pediments were full of curving, elaborate sculpture. A large staircase takes a low, long passage up to the first floor before splitting into two and reversing direction up to the next level. The balustrade and the banister are both decorated with statues depicting all the continents, and Apollo and the zodiac.

Pastels, white, and gold are used throughout the building. The main room, called the Imperial Hall, is two stories with a vaulted ceiling in an oval shape, which was popular in Baroque and Rococo buildings. In this room, stucco entablatures are painted to look like marble. Large, three-dimensional gilded stucco curtains that appear to be held back on the sides by white carved cupids serve as dramatic frames for the frescoes at each end of the room. The ceilings and walls are so decorated that it is difficult to tell where one ends and the next begins, which creates the illusion of an actual sky.

ROMANTICISM AND PICTURESQUE

The Power of Nature

The artistic movement called Romanticism was in many respects a reaction against the rationalism of the Enlightenment and the order and predictability of Neoclassicism. Romantics found imperfect, asymmetrical forms to be beautiful. Whereas Enlightenment thinkers sought to emulate nature and live in harmony with it, Romantics believed that on the whole nature was hostile to man (a popular subject of Romantic painters was storms at sea and shipwrecks).

Picturesque was an aesthetic that accompanied Romanticism. Its adherents saw it as a mediating force between the immense power and horror represented by nature and the notion of beauty embodied in the soft curves of the female body.

Romantic artists and writers were doers. They took up partisan causes and fought for them; the poet Byron, for example, died fighting for the freedom of Greece against the Ottoman Empire. Romantics were also interested in aspects of the human mind, such as the meanings behind dreams and psychological issues. They also wondered about the characteristics of geniuses and heroes.

Among some there was an interest in medieval folk culture. Others were preoccupied with darker themes (in 1818, Mary Wollstonecraft Shelley published *Frankenstein*, one of the first great horror novels). They preferred to honor emotion instead of reason.

Landscape Architecture

William Kent (c. 1685–1748) was one of the founders of English landscape gardening, in which landscapes and gardens are established as a means to improve upon the natural qualities of a property. French gardens were characteristically formal and orderly. The English style, as it evolved in the late eighteenth and early nineteenth centuries, includes looseness and unpredictability. Garden designers worked with the shape of the land, honoring the contours and trees that had already formed. They planned gardens so that the views from the windows were not just of the things they had planted but of the landscape in the distance. The effect was to make the view from the window look like a painting. They might, for example, plan a hedge of boxwoods just so the cows could not come in too near from the pasture. If someone came upon these intentionally sneaky barriers, they might say, "Ah ha!" which inspired the name of the ha-ha, a ditch or wall that forms a boundary in a garden without disturbing the view.

Features of English Landscape Architecture

- Rolling hills: Lawns are better when they have dimension. If a property was flat, designers considered developing manmade mounds.
- Groves of trees: If these did not exist naturally on the property, they should be planted.
- Ruins: These should be set up so that when one looked out the window they could be seen in the distance.
- Ha-ha: A disguised barrier to keep animals from grazing too close to the home and blocking the view of the landscape.

- Lake: A necessary component of landscapes in this period, although most were manmade. It was important that they were developed with irregular shores.
- Grottoes: Manmade caves in the landscape, they suggested romance and mystery.
- Gravel paths: As a guide to visitors so they didn't wander off.

Follies

Often in English gardens, a garden designer would place follies. These were medieval-inspired ruins or structures that served as a visual attraction in the center of a garden. The ruins were manufactured and often invoked a sense of playfulness. Sir Thomas Tresham built the Rushton Lodge as a folly but it was also an opportunity for him to explore and express his love of numbers, which he believed held an intense symbolism. This structure was constructed around the number three. The three is invoked in everything from the three sides of the building to the three holes in the chimney for releasing smoke from the fire.

Horace Walpole (1717–1797) built a folly at Strawberry Hill that was developed by a committee of architects and other artistic and literary friends. The structure is generally Gothic but the interior has some Rococo details such as the chandelier. The interior is also decorated with purple wallpaper. The chimney is adapted from a tomb at Westminster Abbey. There is even pendant vaulting on the interior.

Gothic

A subgenre of Romanticism was Gothic (sometimes spelled "Gothick"). It focused on dark, mysterious themes and primarily found expression in literature. Horace Walpole wrote one of the earliest Gothic novels, *The Castle of Otranto* (1764).

Humphry Repton

Humphry Repton (1752–1818), famed landscape gardener, sometimes placed formal garden elements right up against the houses he was designing. These were intended to smooth the transition between Neoclassical architecture and the landscape. His landscapes were thickly planted, marking his attachment to the Picturesque movement. He would often include terraces and balustrades and steps in his properties.

Repton would paint watercolors of the grounds of a potential client and then make overlays with various ideas for modifications, similar to what a landscape architect might do if he visited your house today.

Influence on American Landscape Design

Inspired by these principles, eighteenth- and nineteenth-century American landscape designers often placed formal gardens, terraces, tennis courts, and swimming pools around the perimeter of country houses. These were offset by the wilder natural landscape beyond. At Jefferson's home in Monticello, the gardens frame grand vistas of Virginia hills that stretch endlessly into the distance.

NEOCLASSICISM
Resurgence in Ancient Styles

In the middle of the eighteenth century, a group of artists emphasized the art and architecture of ancient times. They delved deeper than any revivalists before them to understand the achievements of the ancient civilizations; this meant studying life in antiquity and digesting the history behind different cultures.

The movement was stimulated in part by the expansion of archaeological projects. Books were being published about ancient sites and the story behind ruins. Road construction workers in the kingdom of Naples had uncovered the city of Pompeii. Excavations started at several different ancient sites, which provided scholars and architects with more information about Roman building than they had ever had before.

Mount Vesuvius Erupts

In C.E. 79, Mount Vesuvius erupted, sending scorching gases and a cloud of ash so powerful and quick that it buried the towns of Pompeii and Herculaneum. Both cities had been bustling centers of culture and business. The volcanic debris froze them in place. In fact, it was not until the eighteenth century that they were discovered, and because the ash had so perfectly preserved them in the exact moment of the destruction, archaeologists were able to learn about them and their culture.

Descriptions of Egypt

When Napoleon Bonaparte led a military expedition to Egypt in 1798, he took with him a large group of archaeologists and engineers.

They returned and wrote accounts of what they had seen. Napoleon had established the Institut d'Égypte, which was a fraternity of scholars. The institute examined math, physics, political economy, literature, and arts. Napoleon sat in on the meetings and made recommendations. The institute members were drawn to other subjects as well and were soon embarked on their own paths of discovery.

Institute members traveled through the country, examining the Egyptian monuments and temples and then making very precise engineering renderings that they could share with others. All their efforts culminated in a multivolume work called *Description de l'Égypte*, which included detailed information about the discoveries at these ancient sites. These publications were wildly popular, and designers and architects back in Europe were inspired by the drawings in them.

Engravings of Rome

Giovanni Battista Piranesi (1720–1778) created a giant engraved map of ancient Rome in which he illustrated buildings both real and imagined. It was inspiring to many, and he worked on engravings of the ancient ruins until he died.

He also made a series of sixteen etchings called *Le Carceri*, or *The Prisons*. These were illustrations of laborers, but the engravings contained unusual light sources that made them eerie and conveyed a sense of doom. Buildings were half buried; rooms were filled with chains and heavy doors. The workers were busy among architectural features like vaults and arches.

These plates were huge but were produced in large quantities and cheap to own so they were distributed everywhere. Piranesi etched the first set of fourteen plates in the 1740s but then he reissued them in the 1760s and added two more. In that series he made an even deeper contrast between light and dark and made the architectural forms more elaborate. Now the vaults, arches, and stairways seemed to recede. The images were more precise, which made them even more ominous. Later, the Romantic writers were especially fond of these pieces because of their dark implications.

Emerging Eclecticism

Thomas Daniell's *Antiquities of India* and the Jesuit translations of the Koran and Confucius added to the bank of knowledge Europeans were accumulating about the ancient, non-Western world. All of these works would serve as inspiration for architects and push new boundaries in design. So many styles working together would eventually make way for the eclecticism that emerged in the nineteenth century.

Neoclassicism as the French Revolutionary Style

During the French Revolution, people were looking for a style that invoked a political and moral sense of purpose. They were looking for something to express themes of civic duty and public virtue. Neoclassical style provided that by linking back to the days of antiquity when Romans required the same symbolism from their art and architecture. French Neoclassicists became enraptured with the idea of geometry; simple shapes could be used to make entire buildings.

Étienne-Louis Boullée (1728–1799) was an inventive practitioner of Neoclassicism. He worked on a number of projects, including some particularly influential designs that were never even built. Boullée created a cenotaph for Sir Isaac Newton. The structure was a hollow sphere. The top was punctured with little holes so that light shining in would look like the stars in the night sky. A huge lamp on the inside hung from the ceiling, representing the sun.

Federalist Style

The American Revolution presented an opportunity for Americans to break completely with their colonial past. The architecture, often called "Colonial Georgian," still conjured up images of England and the king, which now seemed inappropriate. Not only had the Americans thrown out the foreign oppressors, but they completely threw out the system of monarchy. They developed their own system with a stable form of government and new principles and humanist ideas. This early period of independence needed a new style to accompany it.

Neoclassicism with its Greek and Roman focus was a perfect expression of this new civic spirit. Thomas Jefferson was the portrait of thoughtful, measured Neoclassicism. He was classically educated and owned the first copy of Palladio's *Four Books of Architecture* that ever reached American shores. He lived in Virginia and hated the architecture there which, at the time, was very colonial, stone, and wooden. He said once that the buildings looked like ovens.

He started building his own home in Virginia, Monticello (meaning "little mountain"), with some very classical traditions in mind. These included a portico, a dome, Doric pillars, an octagon plan, and a balustrade. Palladio liked one-story buildings best so Jefferson planned a structure that would look as if it were one story. Jefferson served as the American envoy to France after the revolution, which deepened his appreciation for Neoclassicism. He also visited temple ruins and used that vision for the State Capitol Building in Richmond, Virginia. He modeled the rotunda at the University of Virginia after the Pantheon with its continuous entablature, two layers of windows, pediment-topped ground floor, symmetry, and low, colonnaded buildings, with all the orders represented.

NEOCLASSICISM IN RUSSIA

Establishing a New Look in Russia

At the end of the seventeenth century, Russia did not fit neatly into the rest of Europe. Politically, it was isolated and its society was very conservative. Cultural trends that were happening elsewhere did not fit into the Russian framework. Peter I (1672–1725) was determined to turn this around and cultivate Russia not only as a major European power but also to transform society. He traveled all over Europe learning about trades, factories, and medicine. He soaked up everything he could about European technology and then hired a team of experts to come and teach all of these things to Russian citizens. He decided to build an entire new city, a place where he could cultivate these western European ideals. He was, essentially, building a brand-new culture.

The city he built, St. Petersburg, was also Russia's first important port on the Baltic Sea, a further sign of Peter's overtures to the West. Later renamed Leningrad, it reverted to its original name after the collapse of communism.

Flowering of Russian Culture

There is some debate about Peter the Great's approach to progress. Some say that he suffocated Russia's traditions and pushed it to take on someone else's. By the middle of the eighteenth century, the Russians had developed an elegant and sophisticated society with its own ballet, opera, and painting. Peter the Great encouraged artists by sending them abroad to study and develop their crafts. Even after he had left the throne, his successors continued to bring architects from Europe to develop designs in Russia.

Smolny Cathedral

One of the most extraordinary building projects in the new St. Petersburg was the Smolny Cathedral (1748–1835). It was designed by popular Italian architect Francesco Bartolomeo Rastrelli, and Empress Elizaveta Petrovna (commonly known as Empress Elizabeth) first presided over the project, but it was not completed until the nineteenth century under Czar Nicholas I. It was a blue and white Rococo confection with a Greek-cross plan. The exterior was light and bright with curving lines and arches, pediments and columns. It was a thoroughly European aesthetic but the three onion domes at the top of the structure were characteristic of Russian architectural tradition.

The cathedral was intended to be the central church of a convent, a home for Peter the Great's daughter Elizabeth who had decided to become a nun. After a series of complicated events, she ended up ascending to the throne. When she died, funding ran out and the building was not finished until 1835. By that time Neoclassicism had become the main style in Russia and that influenced the way the interior was completed.

Catherine the Great

Catherine and Peter III had a deeply unhappy marriage. He acted juvenile and she preferred to sit and read. It took them years to produce an heir (some have speculated that the baby's father may have been Catherine's lover). Peter's progressive reform agenda started to aggravate the Orthodox Church. Catherine conspired with her lover and some confidants to stage a coup. She managed to convince Peter to step down and go in peace, but he was strangled a few days later while in the company of some of her cohorts.

While Peter had a complicated relationship with the elite of Russia, Catherine was much beloved by them. She had many friends all over the continent and patronized some of Europe's leading intellectuals, including Voltaire.

Catherine sought to elevate St. Petersburg's role as Russia's hub for cultivating European culture. The city became known as the "window on the West." The architectural style of Neoclassicism, so popular in the eighteenth century, in Russia became transformed into a symbol of autocracy. Catherine hired architects from all over the continent to come and build Neoclassical buildings in St. Petersburg. Her reign marked a true separation from the church architecture of Russia's past.

The General Staff and Ministries Building, St. Petersburg

Carlo Rossi built the General Staff and Ministries Building in 1819–1829 for the Russian Army, Ministry of Finance, and the Ministry of Foreign Affairs. It was designed to celebrate the victory over Napoleon in 1812. A triumphal arch connects the two wings of the building. Above the arch is a large group of sculptures, including a chariot and two warriors. There was much worry that the sculpture would cause the arch to tumble, so the builders decided to cast only the base in iron; the rest was made from copper.

The Hermitage

In 1765 Catherine purchased more than 200 paintings from a merchant in Berlin. By the end of her rule, she had amassed an enormous art collection, more than 2,500 paintings and tens of thousands of other art works: sculptures, currency, porcelain, and sculptures. The Hermitage was built to house these works. Today it is one of the world's biggest and oldest art museums with 3 million pieces of art on display. During Catherine's time the exhibit was not open to the public but it is today.

Catherine as a Proponent of the Enlightenment

Catherine was fascinated by the intellectual currents of the Enlightenment and considered herself to be a compatriot of the movement—seeing no contradiction between the Enlightenment's ideals of human freedom and her own autocratic rule. She heartily supported Russia's education system, writing a lot of books and pamphlets on the topic. She was close friends with Voltaire and other important figures. She even studied opera so that she could try composing it herself.

BENJAMIN HENRY LATROBE

America's First Architect

Benjamin Henry Latrobe (1764–1820) is often recognized as the first architect in America. He was an architect, engineer, and humanist, born in England and raised there and in Germany. He first studied with Neoclassical architect Samuel Pepys Cockerell. It was here that Latrobe developed a fondness for bold geometrical forms and classical detailing. He then studied with John Smeaton who was a renowned civil engineer in England. In his early thirties he left for America, settling in Norfolk, Virginia, and establishing his own private practice. Eventually he was commissioned to design the Bank of Pennsylvania in Philadelphia. Philadelphia, at the time, was a center for all major American architecture.

The Bank of Pennsylvania

Latrobe designed the Bank of Pennsylvania (1798–1801) in a Greek revival style. The structure was remarkable because it was the first building in America to display a Grecian order. There were Ionic porticos and a central dome with an oculus. After he unveiled this style it was copied all over the country, particularly the porticos.

The U.S. Capitol Building

In 1799, Latrobe designed the first American country house, using the Gothic style. He garnered so much attention for this work that in 1803 President Thomas Jefferson appointed him Surveyor of Public

Buildings. In this new role he oversaw many projects in Washington, D.C., the most important of which was the construction of the south wing of the Capitol Building. He would later supervise the construction of the north wing. Latrobe also oversaw the Navy Yard and work that was completed at the President's House (the White House).

After his term as surveyor ended, in 1814 British troops set fire to the Capitol Building. Latrobe was asked to return to Washington so that he could oversee the restoration of the north and south wings of the building. On these public buildings he always worked in the Classical style, which was stately and exuded a sense of importance. In the House and Senate chambers he modified the Classical style to carry a decidedly American motif in ornamentation: he added corncobs and tobacco leaves to the sculptural elements on the columns.

Architect of the Capitol

Since George Washington's presidency there has been a figure who oversees all national landmarks and federal buildings. The Architect of the Capitol (AOC), appointed by the president, is the ranking steward of such important national landmarks as the Capitol, Senate Office Buildings, Supreme Court, Library of Congress, and U.S. Botanic Garden. The job responsibilities of the Architect of the Capitol include development, maintenance, engineering, and construction. The AOC manages any design of the grounds and facilities. One of his most important jobs is to preserve these pieces of historic architecture.

Baltimore Basilica

Toward the end of his life, Latrobe volunteered to design the first Roman Catholic cathedral in the United States. The Baltimore

Basilica (1806–1821) was to become his most celebrated work. He submitted two design plans to the bishop of Baltimore, John Carroll: one based on Gothic style and one on Neoclassicism. Carroll selected the Neoclassical plan.

The building was ultimately very simple and included a sixty-five-foot dome. There was not much ornament, and everything inside the building was plain. Towers were later added by his son, John H.B. Latrobe, although some believe they actually caused some disruption to what was initially a very thoughtfully proportioned design.

Reconceiving American Monuments

Americans take their historical buildings very seriously and making changes to them is often difficult. For example, when President and Mrs. Obama amended the Old Family Dining Room at the White House, people watched carefully. The Obamas wanted to adjust the design to something more contemporary that reflected their tastes. They added contemporary art—especially a 1966 painting by Alma Thomas from Washington Color School. This is the first piece of art by an African-American woman to be displayed in the White House. Michelle Obama coordinated with the Committee for the Preservation of the White House and the White House Historical Association, which funded things like new drapes and wall sconces. The task was to mix abstract art and modern accents preferred by the Obamas so that they appeared in an elegant fashion. The room includes treasured antiques such as an 1800 mahogany table and sideboard that belonged to Daniel Webster. When the work was done, the room was opened for the first time on the White House Tour so everyone could see what had been done. This is good, since ultimately the White House and its rooms belong to all of us.

Latrobe's career was often marred by financial trouble in part due to some of his less-conventional projects with engines. Some also believe that his trusting nature muddled his decision-making. He was overseeing a waterworks project in New Orleans, Louisiana, when he contracted yellow fever and died. He left an indelible mark on architecture, and it was deepened by those he had mentored. His most accomplished pupils were Robert Mills (1781–1855), who designed the U.S. Treasury Building (1836–1842) and William Strickland (1788–1854), who designed the U.S. Mint and the Naval Asylum.

HENRY HOBSON RICHARDSON

Giving America a Look

Henry Hobson Richardson (1838–1886) was born to a wealthy family in Louisiana. He attended the École des Beaux-Arts in Paris until the economic downturn during the Civil War pushed his family to cut off his tuition support. Without their financial help, he was forced to drop out of school. He worked in Paris for a while before returning to Boston where he won a competition for his design for Trinity Church, one of his most famous offerings in the discipline.

The Trinity of American Architecture

It is said that three architects form the principle foundation of American architecture:

- Henry Hobson Richardson
- Louis Sullivan
- Frank Lloyd Wright

Richardson is such a pivotal character in American architecture that he actually has a style named for him: Richardsonian Romanesque. Few styles are named for a specific practitioner. Richardson was one of the first American architects to attend the Beaux Arts in Paris and he applied his training to developing clear and focused plans for all his projects.

He evolved his style by making adjustments to traditional Romanesque, adding heavier horizontal lines, rough stone, deep windows, and bolder columns. He loved medieval buildings and though he had no formal training in the style, he organized his structures with the heavy massing that Gothic Revivalists preferred. Massing is to a building what broad strokes are to a painting. The fact is, if the massing is not correct, no amount of attention to the details can fix it. Richardson's massing was revolutionary in architecture.

Japanese Influence

Richardson's work stood out in part because of its rich simplicity. He was inspired by the concepts in Japanese architecture such as roofs with a low edge and natural materials like rough stone. These same stylistic features would present themselves later in Frank Lloyd Wright's designs.

Trinity Church

Trinity Church in Boston is widely agreed to be the most celebrated building of its time. Built with a Greek-cross plan, the style is eclectic: there are a number of arches over windows and doors that are reminiscent of classical Roman architecture. The towers on either side of the façade invoke a vertical massing, drawing the eye upward as is common of gothic revival style. The central tower is modeled after the lantern tower atop the Old Cathedral in Salamanaca, Spain. The details all work together in harmony, similar to the way Arts and Crafts designs did. The church includes murals on the interior, red clay tiles on the roof, and stained-glass windows. The artist John La Farge designed the murals and stained-glass windows. His innovative stained-glass method involved laying pieces of opalescent glass on top of each other to create new, creamy colors. The resulting look was quite modern and new. Although so many styles are represented, it does not look clunky or historical because Richardson organized them in a delightfully symmetrical and modern presentation.

Richardson was inspired by the abundance of stone in New England, and the Trinity Church is a stone structure built without a steel frame. The ashlar stonework is in warm gray. The lower part of the building is dark, and the top is red. A continuous band of checkerboard goes around the building.

Glessner House

The Glessner House design was powerful because it was so elegant and restrained, almost austere. It was built on Prairie Avenue in Chicago, which was, in the nineteenth century, the very best street to live on in the city. The house was U-shaped, allowing for a sequestered courtyard that shielded the home from the street noise and soot. The walls are pushed as far as they can go to the perimeter of the property in order to make this interior outdoor space as big as possible, forgoing a front or side yard completely. All the main rooms in the house faced this courtyard, as we saw in ancient Mesopotamian cities. There was very little ornamentation on the house except for the stylized foliage on the arch that appears over the front entrance. This house design had a major impact on Louis Sullivan and Frank Lloyd Wright.

Shingle Style

Richardson's work on residences contributed to the Shingle style that was particularly popular in the Northeast. The style is similar to his stone buildings except that they are covered with shingles instead of stone. Shingle-style homes were built with wooden frames and façades and the roofs were covered with shingles. Sometimes the ground floor might be covered in stone or rusticated stone, as was the case with Richardson's William Watts Sherman House (1875) in Newport, Rhode Island. The house boasts several roof lines with a low edge, also known as eaves. The shingled exterior walls are punctuated with dormers and bay windows.

Marshall Field Wholesale Store

Richardson's most celebrated commercial building was the Marshall Field Wholesale Store (1885–1887), a seven-story warehouse in Chicago. The building was erected before the advent of the steel frame so a seven-story building was considered to be very tall. Richardson designed it to emphasize that fact. The building was revered for the rich materials used and its symmetry. There were even rows of windows with arches topping them. There was a skeleton on the interior, but the walls were load bearing. Richardson avoided any highly ornamented design here, which left a very simple and dignified presentation, powerful in the way it stood on the street. The surface of granite and brownstone was monochromatic so the texture is what created the visual interest.

Massing Strategy

Massing makes a big difference in how a building is able to control its own temperature and light—essentially free energy. You need to decide, for example, whether a building will be short and fat or tall and thin. Buildings that do not house a lot of people benefit from tighter floor plans so that they do not lose too much heat to the outdoors. Buildings with a lot of people in them generate a lot of heat themselves. So in the case of a big office building, longer and thinner floor plans are a good fit.

ARTS AND CRAFTS
Embracing Craftsmanship

By the mid-nineteenth century, the Western world was in the throes of the Industrial Revolution. Production levels surged to previously unthinkable levels thanks to power-driven machines. The steam engine lugged finished goods and people all over the country. Factory towns boomed as newly minted urban centers full of workers were sucking in people from the countryside like a vacuum. Sputtering factories and bleak working-class towns now dotted the English landscape. As the economy rattled and hummed to make room for the expanding manufacturing system, mass production soon supplanted the artisan society.

Resentment sickened a number of thinkers and artists who associated the surge in technology with moral decay and the dehumanization of society. Outspoken opponents of industry and capitalism were outraged by the deplorable working conditions of the factory workers and distraught over how the shifting population changed the aesthetic of the region. Many of these social commentators held a romantic nostalgia for the Middle Ages and the spiritual and social values that aligned with those days. They believed mass-produced goods were forcing a decline of artistic standards and that the quality of life for the individual was corroding as a result.

John Ruskin
John Ruskin (1819–1900) was the most popular commentator on art and society in his day, and his work inspired a younger generation of thinkers and artists who would become ardent practitioners

of his philosophies. Ruskin shunned all technological progress, refusing to ride on trains or accept any goods except those that were produced with handheld tools. He was an early advocate of localism, buying goods and materials from local suppliers, and held beauty in craftsmanship as a moral value. Ruskin believed that good design is linked to good society. He saw the factory worker as enslaved by the rhythm of making many things at a quick pace, leaving him no time to take pride in his skills. Ruskin argued that a role of the craftsman was to illuminate the connections between nature and society, to consider the environment and sustainability. Without their kind of influence, society would corrode and the aesthetic of the country would be ruined. Ruskin had a particular interest in architecture and wrote several influential books on the subject. The first, *The Seven Lamps of Architecture*, published in 1849, outlined his convictions about what he believed to be the principles of architecture: truth, power, beauty, life, memory, and obedience. He pushed for a gothic aesthetic and emphasized a dedication to God and beauty.

William Morris

William Morris (1834–1896) was a divinity student at Oxford when he first heard Ruskin speak. He was so inspired by Ruskin's message that he immediately abandoned his studies so that he could pursue architecture and painting. He too was troubled by capitalism and its impact on good society. He believed that working-class people could rise out of their circumstances if they only had nicer things in their houses, so he started a firm, Morris, Marshall, Faulkner, and Company, that employed artist-craftsmen in small workshops where they created textiles, stained glass, furniture, wallpaper, and carpets that would be readily available for a fair price to people with modest incomes. However, in the new context of a mass-production market, his workshop could not make enough or make it fast enough. And, after a while, his products were too expensive for working-class families.

American Craftsman Style

If the English were drawn to Arts and Crafts style out of sentimentality for the past, the Americans adopted it as a bold statement of their new identity. Throughout the 1800s, architecture styles in America mostly mirrored dominant European styles: Victorian, Italian, and Gothic Revival. All that resulted was a kind of mismatched collection of buildings without any cohesion or cultural identity. The rather ornate hodgepodge of style that resulted from this mixing and matching was called Queen Anne style. Americans were desperate to build an American landscape and the Arts and Crafts movement was largely viewed as an opportunity to develop a truly national aesthetic for the first time.

Main Features of Arts and Crafts

- Rectangular shapes
- Appreciation of nature
- Simple forms
- Little ornamentation
- Natural building materials
- Chimneys as a dominant exterior feature
- Handcrafted details
- Interior lightness, open floor plans
- Built-in design features like cabinets and light fixtures
- Low-pitched roofs
- Porches
- Stained glass

Craftsman-style homes swept the country. The varying climates inspired some variations in the design. On the northeast coast, homes had generally been built in Queen Anne style but were now being covered with wooden shingles made from local, natural materials. The bungalow, particularly popular in warmer climates, was another outgrowth of this movement, its inspiration tracing back to the one-level homes with large porches built in nineteenth-century colonial India.

The first bungalows were built as small Queen Anne cottages in California. These homes featured cobblestone foundations and dominant chimneys. The front door opened right into the living room and most boasted both a front porch and a back porch. In that way, they were part of the philosophy of surrounding oneself with nature. In Chicago, the unforgiving temperatures moved Frank Lloyd Wright to modify the Craftsman style a bit more, resulting in his Prairie style.

The American Craftsman movement intended to provide an affordable, beautiful, hand-crafted, natural, light-filled home that would delight and nurture the American family. These homes quickly became a symbol of the American middle class.

Gustav Stickley

After founding *Craftsman* magazine in the United States in the early 1900s, Gustav Stickley (1858–1942) quickly became a leader in Craftsman style in both home and furniture design. His magazine even carried plans for four different "Craftsman" homes: foursquare, colonial, cottage, and stick styles. Stickley positioned bungalows as an affordable luxury for working-class families. Sears also began selling building kits with a similarly styled bungalow. The company shipped the plans and all the precut materials to a buyer's location by train.

These homes dominated the landscape until after World War I when the Ranch became a popular style.

Innovations of American Craftsman Homes

- Windows—These homes were designed to maximize the light in order to minimize the need for external power. Many homes featured a bank of windows or multipaned sash windows that were grouped together.
- Built-in furniture—Cabinetry and eaves built into the interior design showcased the woodworking and craftsmanship that gave these houses their name.
- Efficiency and function—Craftsman homes were smaller than most Victorian houses but their open floor plans made them much more flexible for everyday living. Large front porches compensated for the lesser square footage. The homes included deep eaves that would shield the house from the sun and reroute water from the foundation.

ART NOUVEAU
Nature and Man Intertwined

Art Nouveau, or *Jugendstil* (translated from German as "Youthful Style), began as an artistic statement against industrialization. It was an aesthetic movement in architecture and the decorative arts that drew inspiration from the curvilinear organic forms that appear in nature. Cities were growing fast and society was evolving at breakneck speed alongside them. There was a hodgepodge of building styles. Everything looked cluttered. The Art Nouveau movement sought a youthful, energetic style that could find harmony with the environment.

Art Nouveau reflected a growing interest in psychology, symbolism, and the supernatural. Architects who ascribed to it wanted to bring back good workmanship but also to produce something utterly modern. They looked for inspiration from the inner world of the spirit and psyche. Art Nouveau had an organic quality with floral and plant motifs, curvy women with flowers adorning their hair, birds, flowers, peacock feathers, and insects.

Influences

Japanese art had a major influence on Art Nouveau. At the time (the opening decade of the twentieth century), Japanese goods were popular as exotic alternatives to traditional European styles. Japanese artists such as Katsushika Hokusai created inspirational, bold wood-block prints. Japanese art was preoccupied with nature and organic forms, and European artists embraced these aesthetics. The Japanese influence on Western culture, and European art in particular, was so profound that it earned its own name: Japonism (from the French, *Japonisme*).

Art Nouveau practitioners drew on these images, as well as others. There were echoes of the intricate designs from Celtic and Viking art and even a dash of French Rococo. Artists also looked to the elegant and intricate patterns of Islamic decoration. These artists' hearts were very open to non-European styles. They were just looking for something new and exciting.

At this time women were pushing for greater independence with the right to vote and divorce, and fighting to be more visible in society than they had ever been previously. Art Nouveau depicted beautiful women with a menacing edge. Women were curvaceous and sexual with loose hair and clothing but also looked morally threatening even though they were intertwined with organic nature themes.

Nature and Man Intertwined

Charles Darwin's works *The Origin of the Species* (1859) and *The Descent of Man* (1871) stirred questions about mankind's place in nature. In the first work, Darwin introduced his scientific theories about evolution and natural selection. In *The Descent of Man* he discussed his theories on sexual selection and suggested that humans and apes were descended from a common ancestor. People were intrigued by the possibility that mankind was not above nature but that the two were actually intertwined. The theme of metamorphosis was widely used, as were insects and horticulture.

The World's Fair of 1900

Despite its emphasis on nature, Art Nouveau was mostly an urban trend and Paris was its center. The Exposition Universelle of 1900 was the movement's breakout. Nearly 50 million people visited the fair where they saw many new machines, inventions, and architecture including the Ferris wheel, Russian nesting dolls, diesel engines, talking films, and the first magnetic audio recorder. Siegfried Bing, an art dealer and owner of the gallery La Maison de l'Art Nouveau, which gave the movement its name, showcased interiors, jewelry, furniture, and fabrics. In one tent, American dancer Loie Fuller performed a wild dance that culminated with her metamorphosis into a flower. It was very inspiring to many Art Nouveau artists.

Main Features of Art Nouveau Architecture
- Asymmetrical shapes
- Fluid, curved forms with a whiplash effect
- Curved glass
- Swirling tendrils, botanical-like embellishments
- Mosaics
- Stained glass
- Japanese motifs
- Exposed iron

Hôtel Van Eetvelde

The Hôtel van Eetvelde in Brussels, Belgium, designed by Victor Horta in 1895, is considered to be a triumph in Art Nouveau because it was truly modern without a trace of revival or historical styles. Horta, in particular, embodied the movement's philosophy that designers should reject revival styles and use organic forms from nature as a map for their work. The façade is made of iron, stone, and glass. The middle sections of the building are slightly cantilevered over the ground floor entry. The front is sequestered behind a swirling iron garden gate. The iron frame is visible from the outside and sinuous, organic patterns on the façade are immediately recognizable as the flowery imprint of Art Nouveau. The interior boasts a patterned glass dome. The design is flowing and fluid with details in marble and exotic timbers.

Technology

Some practitioners of Art Nouveau were excited about the advances in technology. They were not opposed to using materials like iron and met the possibilities with open arms. In fact, Art Nouveau architecture was heavy with exposed wrought iron and irregularly shaped pieces of glass. With these materials, which were produced by machines, the architecture took on a more sculptural quality. Hyperbolas (an open curve with two branches) and parabolas (two-dimensional, mirror-symmetrical curve, like a U shape) were often found in windows, entryways, and doors.

Paris Métro Stations

A number of Paris Métro stations serve as excellent examples of Art Nouveau. Designed by Hector Guimard, there are eighty-six of these entrances still in existence. They were constructed with prefabricated glass and metal. Thin, curvilinear lampposts on either side of the entrance look like flower and plant stalks. The ironwork surrounding the opening is elegant, with swirling floral shapes. Even the lettering on the "Métropolitain" sign corresponds to the style. The iron and glass resemble large bean shoots and seed pods.

Gesamtkunstwerk

Art Nouveau practitioners subscribed to a new open philosophy that embraced all crafts as "total works of art," or *Gesamtkunstwerk*, in which buildings and their interiors were described using the same vocabulary. Previously, only painters and sculptures were taken seriously in art communities but now all art forms had merit. It also meant that buildings, furniture, textiles, clothing, and jewelry should all work together in harmony to conform to the principles of the style.

By the time of World War I, Art Nouveau with its highly stylized materials had become very expensive to produce. The style was replaced by Art Deco in the 1920s, a more streamlined modern look.

BEAUX ARTS
Buildings of Grandeur

While Arts and Crafts and Art Nouveau were celebrating technology with modern flair and social commentary, the École des Beaux-Arts was holding fast to the ancient ruins. The Beaux-Arts was the crème de la crème of architectural schools from which graduating was considered a tremendous achievement. *Beaux-Arts* translates to "beautiful arts" in French. The school narrowed in on the aesthetic principles of classical design, particularly the forms developed by ancient Greeks and Romans.

Many American architects went to Paris to study at the Beaux-Arts, bringing this classical sensibility back with them. This time in America and Europe was known as the Eclectic era because both revival styles and early modern styles were blossoming simultaneously. This trend continued up until the Great Depression. Today Beaux Arts is a popular style for prestigious theaters, monuments, and libraries. These are public buildings that hold a certain distinction, like the Paris Opera House or the Library of Congress. The style exudes harmony, dignity, and order. The details are very precise and sophisticated, in line with the school curriculum. The Beaux-Arts was divided into the Academy of Painting and Sculpture and the Academy of Architecture.

Main Features of Beaux Arts Style
- Massive, elaborate structures
- Ostentatious presentations
- Enormous interior spaces

- Symmetrical lines
- Sculptural decoration such as garlands and floral patterns
- Deep cornices and stately columns
- Flat, low-pitched roofs
- Smooth, light-colored stone for exterior masonry

Windows in the Beaux Arts Style

The windows on Beaux Arts–style buildings are often framed by freestanding columns and decorated with classical pilasters. These stately windows are often pedimented, which means they are gabled dormers that are held up by a series of columns. The triangle within the pediment is known as the tympanum. Frequently the tympanum is covered with relief sculpture of scenes from Greek and Roman mythology.

Interiors

The interior railings on balconies and staircases are held in place by balusters or spindles. These rows of repeating balusters are called balustrades. A very grand staircase sometimes forms the center-piece of an entryway.

Often the rooms are organized in a letter H to allow for air circulation and maximize the lighting. No matter the shape, the interior is grand with large rooms and high ceilings.

On the exterior of the buildings, roofs are frequently flat with cornices. Corbels placed at regular intervals hold moldings in place, similarly to brackets. This system of stone moldings also directs rainwater away from the building in the same way a gutter might. Stately columns add symmetry to the form, some engaged, some decorative. Stone is typically ashlar stone laid very close together, although some of the masonry around the entrances might be rusticated, which adds sturdiness to the look of the ground floor. These rusticated stones can be laid with very wide joints between them to accentuate the shape of the stone.

The World's Columbian Exposition

The 1893 World's Columbian Exposition in Chicago staged five imagined cities that were rich with Neoclassical buildings, stately fountains, statues, state-of-the-art sanitation systems, and open green spaces. The effect was a serene city with sophisticated architecture, of which the citizens could be very proud. It was in stark contrast to the reality of cities in the Industrial Age, with their dirt, slums, and constant noise and congestion. Exposition-goers were infatuated with what they saw. They began to wonder if American cities would stand up a little straighter and find prosperity if they looked like this.

In the late 1800s, America was transitioning from a simple agrarian society to a position of power on the world stage. Urban centers pulled people from every direction and nearly half of Americans were living in cities. As the cities got more crowded they were less appealing to the upper classes. Transportation had improved so it was possible to live outside the city where the houses were bigger and the surroundings were nicer. Many people with means moved outside the cities to places such as the north shore of Long Island, the seaside north of Boston, and the Hamptons and Berkshires. The cities started to deteriorate. The working-class lived in squalor in tenement housing, working conditions were terrible, and there was a general feeling of public neglect.

Progressive reformers and activists such as Jacob Riis tried to help the people in these cities, fearing a mass social upheaval like the Homestead Strike of 1892 and the Pullman Strike of 1894. Rural communities were regarded as having more moral virtue than urban areas. The reformers thought that bringing this kind of character into the cities might solve some of the latter's social ills. Out of this philosophy the City Beautiful movement was born.

City Beautiful advocates believed they could improve the city through, well, making it beautiful. They thought that beauty would inspire civic loyalty and create an inviting place for the upper classes to return. They wanted to use beauty as a means to social control. It was the first time Americans took time to thoughtfully consider civic centers and city planning. This enlightened approach to urban design lasted up to the Great Depression when all hope of urban prosperity was destroyed.

Union Station, Washington, D.C.

Union Station was one such building impacted by the City Beautiful movement. The station was built in 1908 after the Pennsylvania Railroad and B&O Railroad decided to come together under one train terminal. Having one large train station would make Washington, D.C. a favored destination and strengthen its position as the capital. Daniel H. Burnham designed the building in the Beaux Arts tradition with marble, gold leaf, white granite, and elaborate statues. The entrance is framed by a triumphal arch. The waiting room is a large marbled room with a ninety-six-foot-high ceiling. Above the main cornice stand six statues of the Dacian prisoners of the Arch of Constantine, slaves taken from the kingdom of Dacia during Trajan's reign in Rome. Burnham used Guastavino tiles, which were fireproof and favored by most Beaux Arts architects. The interior of the station included a full range of services and dining rooms and even a mortuary. The station was positioned on a large green lot that resembled a park.

The Beaux Arts style continues even today. The clothing designer Ralph Lauren recently opened a store in a newly built Beaux Arts building on Madison Avenue and Seventy-second Street in New York City.

GOTHIC REVIVAL

Reacting to the Industrial Age

Gothic is one of the most enduring revival styles of modern history. In the mid-1800s, England was enraptured with the Gothic style in both art and literature. Popular authors such as Horace Walpole and Matthew Lewis thrilled readers with stories about dark and mysterious characters. Mary Shelley wrote *Frankenstein*, John Polidori wrote *The Vampyre*, and in 1897 an Irish author, Bram Stoker, published the most famous vampire novel ever, *Dracula*. In architecture, John Ruskin emphasized the quality of medieval craftsmanship in comparison to industrially produced widgets. In art, a new aesthetic style called Picturesque depicted medieval times as the golden age of art (see Romanticism and Picturesque). There was a keen interest in preserving and renovating medieval architecture.

Augustus Welby Northmore Pugin

In Britain, one of the most popular architects was an intense Gothic Revivalist named Augustus Welby Northmore Pugin (1812–1852). Pugin, a passionate gothic revivalist, designed many things besides buildings; he made tiles, metalwork, furniture, wallpaper, stained glass, and ceramics, all dedicated to the style of the Middle Ages. He argued that only members of a good society can make things that are honest and beautiful. He was convinced that the current times were devoid of virtue. He produced drawings that compared towns the same towns as they looked in the mid-1400s to the way they looked during his time in the mid-1800s. He showed how what were once provincial towns with green space, blue skies, and church spires had devolved into gray, smoky, factory-ridden cities. Pugin showed monasteries from medieval times juxtaposed with working-class tenement housing. He presented a crude picture of overdevelopment. He believed that reinstituting Gothic style could correct the ugliness.

Choosing a Style for British Parliament

One of Pugin's best-known projects was his collaboration on the new Houses of Parliament after the old buildings were destroyed by fire in 1834. There was considerable debate at the time over whether the new Parliament should be built in Classical or Gothic style but, in the end, Gothic prevailed because it was believed to embody the national spirit and Christianity. As well, the basis of the parliamentary system had been established during the Middle Ages so having a building that nodded toward that history provided a link to this fact.

St. Augustine's Church, Ramsgate

Pugin designed a number of churches and cathedrals around England. He was obsessed with lively and historically correct details. He designed a church in honor of St. Augustine that he donated to the Roman Catholic Archdiocese of Southwark. The interior was made of ashlar masonry that was carved under his total supervision. He built his own house next door. That house included a crenellated tower, gables, and bay windows. The biggest innovation was large open interior space that included both horizontal and vertical lines. This feature was widely influential; you can especially see it in Frank Lloyd Wright's work.

Features of Gothic Revival

- Reminiscent of medieval style
- Ornate corner gables
- Finials
- Scalloping

- Gargoyles and spires as ornamentation
- Strong vertical lines that give a sense of great height
- Pointed arch windows
- Pinnacles

Inspiration from Medieval Security Systems

One medieval innovation that inspired some features in Gothic Revival architecture was the battlement. A battlement involved a parapet or low wall—about chest or head height—with squared notches cut out of the stone at regular intervals. These gaps were called crenels and they allowed for someone to fire an arrow or other ammunition through them. In the Gothic Revival style, of course, battlements were purely decorative.

Carpenter Gothic

Ralph Adams Cram (1863–1942) led the Gothic Revival in America, which was initially reserved mostly for churches and home residences. Often it was used in rural settings because the features were difficult to squeeze into tight city lots. Wood and timber was abundant in the United States so they became a popular alternative to stone as building materials. In the northeast, Gothic Revival homes were built with wood frames, which inspired the term *Carpenter Gothic*. These homes featured steeply pitched roofs and pointed arch windows, which drew the design even further upright. Often such a home might have a number of gables. They were quaint and plain and mostly unadorned (the style was exemplified in the famous Grant Wood painting, *American Gothic*). The only ornamentation was intricate pieces of carved molding that lined the roofs and porches, like the lace found on gingerbread. The look came together as intimate and charming, in stark contrast to the strong and pious stone churches most typical of the Gothic Revival movement.

The Steam-Powered Scroll Saw

The invention of the steam-powered scroll saw in the nineteenth century allowed for mass production of detailed and intricate pieces of molding that appeared on Carpenter Gothic structures. The ability to mass produce the most ornate feature on these homes helped to keep the prices low. These houses, in turn, appealed to people at all levels of society.

In the twentieth century, Gothic Revival style was considered impractical. The popularity of functionalism and the availability of new building materials caused it to fade.

FRANK LLOYD WRIGHT

Modern Elegance

Many consider Frank Lloyd Wright to be the greatest architect of the twentieth century. His designs were so innovative that it can be confusing to look at, say Fallingwater and know that it was built in the mid-1930s rather than later. Wright's overbearing mother determined even before he was born that he would be an architect. His father was a musician and preacher and the family moved often when he was a boy. When his parents divorced he settled permanently with his mother in Wisconsin. Young Wright fell in love with the woodsy scenery and spent a lot of time exploring outdoors.

High school did not appeal to him nearly as much so he dropped out and took a job at the University of Wisconsin working as an office boy for a civil engineering professor. He took some classes too, but school still did not appeal to him. He decided to drop out and head to Chicago to get a job—and not just any job. He set out to work for the influential firm of Adler and Sullivan, which was one of the most premier firms in the country. He pushed hard and was hired. Wright thrived at Adler and Sullivan, and it was not long before he assumed responsibility for most of the firm's residential commissions, among them the famous Charnley House in Oak Park, Chicago.

Wright's work was growing in popularity and he took on a lot of commissions, even some outside of Adler and Sullivan. Eventually Adler and Sullivan fired him for breach of contract and he took that opportunity to start his own firm.

Prairie Style

Wright had spent much time developing residential properties in the Chicago suburbs. Prairie style was born out of his attempt to inject Midwestern character into the homes he was designing. He realized that he preferred homes that sat close to the ground and had a horizontal composition much like traditional Japanese homes. He liked the elegance of a home developed in harmony with the landscape.

How Prairie Style Embraced the Midwest

- Long hanging eaves over windows kept out the hot Chicago summer sun but let in low winter rays to heat the house.
- The fireplace was situated at the core of the house to heat the home.
- The exterior was designed to fit into the landscape, whether a woodsy lot in a rural setting or a small lot in the city.
- Gardens were often sequestered to provide some relief from dirt and traffic on the busy streets.
- Local materials were used whenever possible.
- Horizontal lines and low-pitched roofs echoed the flat landscape.

Organic Architecture

Wright's style was dubbed "organic architecture" because he emphasized the importance of humans living in harmony with nature rather than conquering the environment. He maintained two main approaches to domestic architecture:

1. A house should blend in with its environment.
2. The interior and exterior of a house should be integrated both visually and physically.

Robie House, Chicago

Robie House (1909) in Chicago, built in Prairie style, was a three-story house that was built on a long plane. Wright emphasized symmetry and openness. The fireplace, in the second story living room, was the core of the home. The dining room and living room were also situated on the second floor, extended by terraces that opened the space up further and allowed room for ventilation. These spaces were covered by large cantilevered roofs that blocked the summer sun. The bedrooms were on the third floor. The playroom and service quarters are on the lowest level. Wright emphasized rectilinear spaces, which makes the exterior seem very long and low. The façade was made with brick and natural wood. The interior was fitted with the latest developments in heating, lighting, and furniture. Since he was always thinking of the outdoors, Wright took particular care designing windows. He seemed to defy gravity, wrapping glass around corners and using long bands of windows to light interior space. In the Robie House, he also included a band of stained-glass windows with clear panes and occasional pops of color that emphasized geometric shapes; this design softened the light that entered the home.

He was firm in his beliefs that the inside and outside of a home should be cohesive, and even designed the interior furniture to make sure that everything blended.

Usonian Houses

After many years of achievement, Wright's personal life took some complicated twists and turns. He left his wife and six children to run off with a client's wife who left her family too. After loafing around Europe, they returned to the United States, where he built a home for them. However, one day one of the servants set the house on fire and murdered seven people inside, including Wright's girlfriend and two of her children. All of these things distracted Wright from his work for a long time.

When he started producing again, his output was incredible. One of his design projects was a series of sixty middle-income homes called Usonian houses that were essentially the precursor to Ranch style. These homes, the first of which was built in 1936, were sparse and elegant. They were outfitted with revolutionary energy methods including solar heating and natural cooling. They also had carports and were made of prefabricated wood panels that were intended to be easily assembled on top of a concrete base.

Fallingwater

The home Wright designed in 1935 for the Kaufmann family from Pittsburgh is his masterpiece. Set in Bear Run, Pennsylvania, a wooded area next to a stream and a small but beautiful waterfall, the house was built mostly from stone that had been quarried from the immediate area. Fallingwater includes three horizontal terraces made from reinforced concrete, two of which cantilever over the waterfall. It looks death defying, but the concrete has a high tensile strength that makes it stay rigid and strong. The terraces were built to resemble the stone ledge in the waterfall. At that time, it was unusual to see a cantilever on a home.

The interior of the house uses an open floor plan with one large room that opens out to the terraces. Here Wright emphasized the "organic" flow of space, forgoing walls because he thought they would be too disruptive. His standard massive fireplace was situated in the middle. Of course he also designed the interior furniture.

The Guggenheim, New York

Late in life, Wright began work on a number of public buildings, the most famous of which is the Guggenheim Museum in New York City. The design was controversial for 1943, the year it was commissioned. He envisioned a building where "art will be seen as if through an open window." A single gallery runs along a ramp that curves up continuously from the ground floor to a Plexiglas dome at the top. Critics complained this was not an acceptable way to view art because you can actually see other works besides the exhibit you are supposed to be looking at. The walls gradually taper inward as the ramp gets closer to the ceiling. Wright's design was thought of as an inverted ziggurat, like the ones in ancient Mesopotamia. It is now regarded as one of New York's finest buildings, but Wright never got to see it because he died six months before it was even built in 1959.

LOUIS HENRY SULLIVAN

The Father of Skyscrapers

Louis Henry Sullivan (1856–1924) was sixteen when he was accepted at MIT but he attended for only a year before accepting a position working for Frank Furness, a Victorian-era architect who designed hundreds of buildings in Philadelphia. It was not long before the depression of 1873 squelched the building opportunities in Philadelphia and Sullivan had to leave his job. He decided to join the herd of other young architects who rushed to Chicago after the Great Fire of 1871 to look for new opportunities. He found a job almost immediately working for William Le Baron Jenney, the mastermind behind the Home Insurance Building, which was largely considered to be the first skyscraper. After his time in Chicago, Sullivan went to Paris where he studied at the École des Beaux-Arts.

The Auditorium Building

When Sullivan returned to the United States he partnered with Dankmar Adler, and together they won a series of theater commissions. One of their most admired theaters was the Auditorium Building in Chicago (1887–1889), a tall structure that was the first ever to be used for multiple purposes and businesses. For that time, this was a brand-new concept. The remarkable complex included a 4,200-seat theater, a hotel, an office building, and storefronts on the ground level. Adler was experienced in acoustical engineering so the theater had state-of-the-art sound quality. They also installed electric lighting and air conditioning, which further established it as one of the more technologically innovative buildings of its time. It even included fireproofing features throughout the entire structure.

The Auditorium Building was massive. It had been constructed with a shell structure, meaning the stones were stacked on top of each other. It showed the way in which Sullivan was influenced by Richardson's Marshall Field Wholesale Store (see Henry Hobson Richardson). The ground level boasts three strong arches reaching over the entryways. Just above them sits a cantilevered block of windows, behind which is the hotel lobby. The building has a vertical composition with long horizontal rows of windows that are separated by thick columns that stretch up the middle of the building, drawing the eye upward.

The Wainwright Building

In 1890, Adler and Sullivan won their second commission for a tall building, one that was intended to be an office building: the Wainwright Building in St. Louis, Missouri. At that point, many architects had started using steel frames but they were still nervous about whether a skeleton-and-skin building was safe. Even though the column-style steel frames were doing all the work to secure the structure, architects continued to place massive heavy stone in front of the frame to ensure that everything looked sturdy and wide.

Sullivan was bold. He did not waste time with the heavy stones. Instead, he designed a building that emphasized the height and lightness of the building. He worked with bays of windows stretched horizontally across each of the seven office floors, each separated by strong vertical piers. He placed dominant piers at each of the four corners of the building to showcase the height.

Even the color of the building was bold in red brick, granite, and terra cotta. It was constructed with a very modern style but Sullivan gave a nod toward some of the classical conventions in which he had been well trained. The composition was tripartite, inspired by a classical column. The roof was capped with a heavy cornice and just below it a large frieze decorated with a leafy motif. The frieze was pierced with the occasional bull's-eye window behind which the elevator machinery and water tanks were housed. The spandrels were also decorated in a leafy pattern.

Sullivan believed firmly that the design of a building should reflect its use. He touted that famous maxim, "Form ever follows function." He believed that a person walking by the building on the street should be able to determine what went on in the Wainwright Building just by looking at it.

The Chicago School

Sullivan's inventive approach to tall buildings earned him the title "the father of skyscrapers." He inspired countless followers including Frank Lloyd Wright, whose Prairie style draws on some of Sullivan's guiding principles. Sullivan's modern aesthetic was so influential that much of Chicago's new architecture began to take on a similar look and demeanor. Collectively, this style became known as the Chicago School. One of the most recognizable features of the Chicago School style is the three-part windows. Each includes a fixed center pane that is flanked by sash windows on either side. These side windows can slide open for ventilation.

Features of the Chicago School
- Steel frames
- Swirling, circular patterns for ornamentation
- Terra cotta detailing
- Neoclassical features
- Composition similar to the three parts of a classical column

Winning a Commission

Typically, architects earn commissions by winning them. A major funder, or a city government, or a company owner—whoever is paying for the project—will put out an open call for proposals. They will describe their general vision, the main function of the building, and any technical considerations like the environment at the site or city codes with which the structure must comply. Then they will provide the specific criteria on which the proposal will be judged. When the winner is selected, usually by a jury, they are then awarded with a contract.

SKYSCRAPERS

America Leads the Way to the Sky

There were three major developments that paved the way for architecture to head skyward: the 1871 Chicago Fire, the development of the steel frame, and the invention of the electric-powered elevator.

The Chicago Fire

By the late 1800s Chicago had long shrugged off any doubts about whether it deserved a seat at the table of the great American cities. It stood between the two coasts and proved that you do not need access to an ocean to make something of yourself. The railroad now stretched across the entire United States and Chicago was a major hub between the agricultural regions in the west and the manufacturing boom in the east. When the fire started on October 10, 1871, somewhere in the vicinity of Mrs. O'Leary's barn, Chicago was a very crowded place. It was crammed with over 1,000 factories, commercial traffic, houses, wooden sidewalks, municipal buildings, and a huge stockyard. Its economy had grown faster than any deliberate—or even responsible—civil planning could keep pace with. On that hot night, a stretch four miles long and three-quarters of a mile wide burned to the ground. An unfathomable number of homes and business burned, somewhere around 18,000 buildings. In the newspapers, people compared it to the destruction at Pompeii.

When it was over, though, the most critical portion of the railroad was still mostly intact. The stockyard was still functioning. The people stayed. One hundred thousand people needed new homes and, heavens knows how many needed places to go to work.

Chicago lurched out of the ashes. Soon it was regarded as a place of opportunity. Real estate boomed and developers and businessmen clamored for space in the middle of the city. Young architects and engineers raced after them to cut their teeth on all the demand. And when space got tight to the sides, they started to use the space above.

Skeleton-and-Skin System

Before we even get into the beautiful buildings that came out of the first rush of skyscrapers, it is important to understand how it was even possible to stack multiple floors without them crumbling underneath the weight of one another.

Every home, building, or temple we have discussed from the Stone Age up until this point can be placed into one of two categories: shell structure or skeleton-and-skin structure. In a shell structure the walls support the weight of the entire building. The walls, in that case, operate both as structural support and as a boundary from the outside. The skeleton-and-skin system uses a strong material for structural support and a lighter material for the walls.

SHELL STRUCTURES	SKELETON-AND-SKIN STRUCTURES
Log cabin	Mammoth bone huts
Mud brick house	Wigwam
Pyramid	Wooden-framed shingle-style homes

For centuries, skeleton-and-skin seemed like a more primitive approach to construction. That is, until an inventive greenhouse designer named Joseph Paxton came along. In 1851, Prince Albert of England hosted an exhibition in Hyde Park. It was called the Works of Industry of All Nations. Paxton constructed an enormous, mind-bending structure from glass and cast iron that was seventeen acres wide and 108 feet high. Visitors were completely flummoxed. The height and the transparency of the building were so alien to them that they could not understand what they were seeing. The glass seemed to bend over the cast iron like it was ... skin. This changed everything because now it was clear that as long as the skeleton was very strong you could sheath it with anything, even something as fragile as glass.

The Steel Frame

Conveniently, just as these possibilities were dawning on architects and city planners, the price of steel was down in the United States and mass production was widespread in industry. Steel was fashioned into a very strong column-frame. The skin, known as the curtain wall, made from terra cotta or brick, was suspended from the frame. The windows were then hung in each section of curtain wall. Steel is strong in that it can hold distributed weight but also has tensile strength, which means it can handle a certain degree of longitudinal stress such as that produced by wind.

If you want to get a good look at a steel frame that is not hiding behind a sheath, look at the Eiffel Tower. Now a ubiquitous symbol of Paris and romance, the Eiffel Tower was a technological marvel when it was built (1887–1889). Some people even thought it was offensive-looking. Alexandre Gustave Eiffel, the mastermind behind the Statue of Liberty, designed the open-latticework tower that shot up over a base of reinforced concrete. It stands on four arched columns that curve inward to meet in one single column that reaches 1,063 feet into the sky and offers a fifty-mile panoramic view of Paris. It stands rigid against all the elements and the wear and tear of countless tourists who are hoisted to the top in one of eight different elevators each day.

The Electric Elevator

Hundred-story buildings would never have worked if the people who entered them had been expected to climb the stairs. The elevator had been around since the beginning of the twentieth century, hauling coal and lumber from worksites. The passenger elevator, however, was a tremendous luxury with automatic doors, acceleration control, and safeties. The presence of an elevator also meant that buildings needed to be fitted with shafts that ran from the lowest to the highest levels—an extra-wide shaft if it was to include enough room for multiple elevators running at once.

The Empire State Building

The first skyscraper was the Home Insurance Building in Chicago with ten stories. More quickly followed, such as the Rand McNally Building in Chicago (1889–1911). It was also a ten-story building structured with an all-steel frame. Inside, it was fitted with several hundred offices and more than a dozen stores. There was the Reliance Building (1892–1895) at fourteen stories. After ground broke on the Reliance Building, city leaders started to get nervous about what all these tall buildings might do to the look and feel of Chicago. They decided to place a ten-story limit on all future buildings as a precaution.

New York City was much less queasy about the thought of skyscrapers taking over the landscape because the city government had developed zoning regulations to keep a minimum of light and air at the street level. For example, they required buildings to have setbacks, as a way to ensure that the areas in front of the buildings remain wide. The Empire State Building (1929–1931) by William Lamb of Shreve, Lamb, and Harmon quickly became to New York

City what the Eiffel Tower is to Paris: a cultural emblem recognizable to almost anyone in the world.

It was built to be tall; especially taller than the Chrysler Building. John Jacob Raskob, then head of General Motors, was determined to develop a tower to rival his toughest competitor. The steel beams came from a mill in Pittsburgh and were fitted together onsite. Built in Art Deco style with brick, concrete, and limestone, the recessed walls contributed to the sleek geometric lines. Lamb fitted the core with multiple elevators and an observation deck at the top. It remained the world's tallest building until the early 1970s when the World Trade Center was erected.

New York's Top 10 Skyscrapers

BUILDING	HEIGHT
Woolworth Building (1910–1913)	60 stories
American Standard Building (1924)	23 stories
Chrysler Building (1928–1930)	77 stories
Empire State Building (1929–1931)	102 stories
30 Rockefeller Center (1931–1933)	70 stories
United Nations Headquarters (1947–1953)	39 stories
Seagram Building (1954–1958)	38 stories
The Lipstick Building (1983–1986)	34 stories
Hearst Tower (2003–2006)	46 stories
Freedom Tower (2006–2014)	104 stories

ART DECO

Embracing Technology and Mass Production

Like Art Nouveau and the Arts and Crafts movement before it, Art Deco was the product of an attempt to find something utterly modern. This style was a direct departure from the organic motifs featured in Art Nouveau. Art Deco advocated instead developed designs that embraced industry and exuded a faith in the technological and social constructs of the day. Proponents of Art Deco wanted to demonstrate glamour and luxury as a way to announce the dark days were over and there was a new prosperity. They were inspired by mass production, as well as by a cultural shift. Prohibition had ended and girls were making feminist statements by cutting their hair and dressing in shorter skirts. Morale was high and the future looked bright.

Art Deco emphasized luxury and newness with reflective materials like chrome, steel, and glass. Geometric patterns with strong lines and clear symmetry accented both interior and exterior surfaces. It was stylish and current, bucking revivalist tendencies in architecture to draw inspiration from the moment. The style first appeared at *L'Exposition internationale des arts décoratifs* in Paris in 1925.

Cubism

Cubism made an impact on several forms of architecture. Cubist artworks try to show paintings from multiple viewpoints. To do so, the objects depicted are broken up and reassembled. Eyes on a single face might look slightly different from each other, for example. The style was developed largely by Pablo Picasso (1881–1973) and Georges Braque (1882–1963). Architects were interested in the way it emphasized simple design and abstract presentation of objects without classical reference.

Art Deco as American Style

American architects believed Art Deco to be an important way to inject character into the American skyscraper. The Chrysler Building (1928–1931) is a magnificent example of Art Deco with its shiny top of stainless steel glinting in the sun and tiered arches lined with sunbursts on the prominent 185-foot tower top, or spire.

Walter Chrysler, founder of Chrysler Motors Corporation, wanted to build a symbol of his company's prosperity that would be recognizable all over the city. He asked architect William Van Alen (1883–1954) to build something even taller than the Eiffel Tower. When it appeared there was a chance that the building might be outrivaled by a bank tower on Wall Street, Van Alen quietly built the famous 185-foot spire inside the building. When it was done, he hoisted it up through the roof, shocking everyone.

The building takes a streamlined approach to form with geometric patterns and stylized ornaments such as the stern-looking steel eagles that look out over the top of the building like gargoyles. These eagles mimic Chrysler's hood ornaments. The spire glints with its stainless steel and triangular shapes punched into the aluminum arches that form the spire. The shaft is glazed brick with dark trim. The frieze is a series of simulated hubcaps—nods toward the Chrysler business. The interior is luxurious with red-hued Moroccan marble and exotic wood inlay decorating all the doors, including those of the thirty-two elevators.

Features of Art Deco Architecture
- Rich colors
- Bold geometric shapes
- Lavish ornamentation
- Symmetry
- Rectilinear forms
- Clean, streamlined forms

Art Deco as a Revival Style

A revival of Art Deco known as Streamline Moderne occurred during the Great Depression and ended before World War II. Miami, a fairly new American city that was already experiencing a building boom, was in need of a look. This second wave of Art Deco took strong roots there. Streamline Moderne was more subdued than the original Art Deco, tempered by the economic downturn of the Great Depression. It was less decorative but used bright pastels, and ornamentation included glass blocks, floral images, and ship motifs.

Some people even called it Tropical Deco. Whatever its name, there was a certain optimism to the look. Common features included rounded edges, porthole windows like those that appear on ships, stepped roofs, and neon lighting.

Streamline Moderne in Transportation

Streamline Moderne was not just an architecture style. It was also used in automobile design, ships, and many household appliances such as refrigerators. It was influenced by modern aerodynamic principles.

Beginning in 1929, the Great Depression brought an end to the exotic, luxurious ornamentation of Art Deco, replacing it with a more austere, streamlined style. In light of the financial crisis, the original Art Deco style exuded a decadence that seemed frivolous and inappropriate.

THE BAUHAUS
Refining German Design

Following World War I, Germany was a disaster. The economy was in a slump, many young men had been killed in the fighting, and industrial production was suffering. There was a growing sentiment that embracing industry might actually raise the quality of German design and improve the situation.

In 1919, architect Walter Gropius was promoted to lead an educational institution that would combine a school of Arts and Crafts with a fine arts academy. Named the Bauhaus (translated as "House of Construction"), the curriculum was modeled after the medieval guilds in that apprentices worked to earn journeyman's certificates. Students took craft workshops and studied theory. The professors were often painters. In fact, Wassily Kandinksy (1866–1944) was a member of the faculty for more than ten years. Gropius saw the curriculum as being in direct contrast to the Beaux Arts tradition.

Sample Bauhaus Courses

- Study of Form and Theory of Materials
- Study of Nature
- Study of Materials
- Composition Study
- Space Study
- Glass
- Clay
- Stone
- Textiles
- Building Design

The Bauhaus philosophy was that the best product would come from an interdisciplinary effort. Everyone from the fine artists to architects worked together from planning through construction. They respected the synergy between the individual and modern society but they rejected any style elements that seemed too classical or fancy.

Walter Gropius

Gropius had a strong background in architecture. For one thing, his father was an architect as was his great uncle, renowned Berlin architect Martin Gropius. One of his first jobs was as an assistant to the famous architect Peter Behrens (1868–1940). Behrens was particularly invested in the effort to bring an industrial angle to traditional design. He designed the AEG Turbine Factory in Berlin, a classically inspired building that exuded power and reverence for industry. Gropius then set up a firm with Adolf Meyer. Their first major commission was the Fagus Factory at Alfeld-an-der-Leine. The building boasted extremely innovative design details that later became associated with International style: glass curtain walls that were supported by a steel framework topped by a flat roof. The building looked quite modern, in part because there was no solid masonry or decoration visible on the exterior. Gropius was inspired by Frank Lloyd Wright. Things were going well but then he had to put his own work on hold in order to serve in World War I. After the war, Gropius thought a lot about what it would take to rebuild Europe efficiently. He was preoccupied with how to develop well-planned housing that was visually appealing but also respectful of the post-war environment.

Features of Bauhaus Buildings

- Flat roofs
- Smooth façades
- Cubic shapes
- Muted approaches to color: white, gray, beige, black
- Open floor plans
- Functional furniture
- Steel frame
- Glass curtain walls

The Bauhaus Workshop

As the Bauhaus aged, conflicts with its administration became complicated. Flamboyant faculty and a political student body were becoming the subject of much interest beyond architecture. The finances of the school began to decline, and it came under increasing scrutiny from the Nazis. Gropius tried desperately to put things back on track. He fired the rowdy faculty and moved the campus from Weimar to Dessau. He started selling plans for items that could be mass produced.

Despite Gropius's best efforts, eventually the Nazis prevailed and destroyed the school, which they believed to be a decadent expression of communist values.

American International Style

When the Nazis rose to power and the Bauhaus collective disbanded, many of the leading architects were reunited in the United States where they resumed their efforts in the Modern movement. For the first time, the United States took the lead in architectural theory and design. The American extension of Bauhaus became known as International style. It shed the connections to social politics and instead aligned itself with the parameters of capitalism. Today it is the preferred style for office buildings and upscale luxury homes. By the mid-twentieth century, American International style had evolved to accommodate the vast array of climates and terrain across the United States. Even small regional identities began to form, such as Desert Modernism, which was popular in dry climates like California and areas of the Southwest.

United Nations Secretariat Building

This is probably the best contemporary example of International style. It was designed by a team of international architects including Le Corbusier (1887-1965), Oscar Niemeyer (1907-2012), and Wallace Harrison (1895–1981). The International style symbolized the new start after the war. Completed in 1952, it was New York's first true green glass curtain wall building. It stands thirty-nine stories and uses reinforced concrete and aluminum for the details on the exterior. This was the first major International-style building in New York, characterized by its simple geometric forms and devoid of any historical ornamentation. The building helped to revitalize midtown Manhattan in the 1950s.

TOWARD A NEW ARCHITECTURE

Le Corbusier Pushes the Limits of Modern Aesthetic

Le Corbusier, as he referred to himself, was born Charles-Édouard Jeanneret-Gris in a watchmaking town in Switzerland. He received formal education at the local Arts and Crafts school where he learned to engrave watch cases. His teachers were impressed with his abilities and encouraged him to press on to a bigger art form. So he went to work for architects Auguste Perret and Peter Behrens. Perret was a pioneer in using reinforced concrete for construction. Behrens was already famous for his innovations in Industrial Classicism style. Le Corbusier also took time to see some inspiring sights, traveling around the Mediterranean and Greek Isles before returning to Switzerland to teach and work.

The House Machine

Le Corbusier's first major commission was the Dom-ino House (1914–1915). The building was a statement about World War I. He assumed that the fighting would destroy everything and that it would all have to be rebuilt when the war finally ended. To make all of that easier, he proposed an easily replicated house form that could be mass produced. He reduced the design elements to the absolute bare minimum. The Dom-ino House, for example, had bare floor slabs. There were unadorned columns placed regularly for vertical support. The floors were connected by simple stairs. Using prefabricated parts meant that the whole house could be quickly assembled right on the lot. Some things would be left up to the creative discretion of the builder onsite, including the walls and the way the interior was subdivided into rooms.

Armed with his new ideas, Le Corbusier moved to Paris. In France, he was not well known and there was not a lot of available work because of the war, so he spent his days painting, writing, and drawing. During this time he developed a magazine with painter Amédée Ozenfant and poet Paul Dermée called *L'Esprit Nouveau*, which was dedicated to the "modern aesthetic." His essays were, by the day's standards, pretty radical. In them, he linked Greek temples and Gothic cathedrals with modern innovations such as cars, ocean liners, and airplanes. He brought them all together in the context of "new architecture." He also talked about his ideas for mass-produced houses; he argued that the house is a machine in which people can live.

Towards a New Architecture

In what was essentially his manifesto, *Towards a New Architecture*, Le Corbusier stated that the mass produced house could be as beautiful as the implements of the industry that were used to build it.

He presented his style at the Art Deco Show in Paris in 1925. His futurist designs emphasized geometry. The buildings were stark white with abstract modular components that stood out against nature. This represented his version of the International style.

Five Points

Le Corbusier wrote a declaration of the five basic tenets that he believed made up the new architecture. He firmly believed that studying historical architectural forms was not enough.

1. Using poles to elevate the building from the earth allows for the garden to extend underneath without interruption.
2. A roof should be functional so that it can be used as both a garden and a terrace. A roof garden can be elaborate with flowerbeds and trees—in fact, this would protect the concrete roof from the changing weather patterns. This would also serve to recover the land that the house was built upon.
3. The interior floor plan should be free and open without load-bearing walls. This leaves the opportunity to place partitions only if and where they are aesthetically pleasing.
4. Instead of vertical windows, which were a prominent style of most architecture, Le Corbusier argued that long horizontal windows provided the best illumination and ventilation. These windows would light a room from end to end.
5. Façades should serve only as the skin of the wall and to hold windows because they do not have any load-bearing responsibilities.

Villa Savoye

Villa Savoye (1929–1931) was a Modernist villa in Poissy-sur-Seine on the outskirts of Paris. It was a vision of Le Corbusier's beliefs about the possibilities of mass production in domestic living. The floors were made of concrete slabs and were supported by vertical concrete pillars. Multiple floors were linked by stairs and the roof was flat. The columns that held the structure up from the foundation also divided the second-floor windows. The ground floor was very compact beneath the main living area on the second floor. This lowest level included the entrance hall. From there a ramp led up all the way to the third floor. The villa was extremely influential in the International Modern movement.

Notre-Dame du Haut Chapel

In the 1940s, Le Corbusier began to experiment with new materials. He became less focused on mass production and more centered on symbolic design. New Brutalism, as an outgrowth of the International style, was a reform movement that advocated the return to functionalist principles and, in doing so, avoiding polish and elegance in building structures. He left concrete rough and unfinished as it is in its natural form. Le Corbusier capitalized on the sculptural qualities of concrete, as evidenced by his Notre-Dame du Haut Chapel in Ronchamp, France (1950–1955). This chapel was a complete departure from the five points of his earlier work. This building intended to be a statement that the church was swearing off decadence and embracing Modernism. This was a place for spiritual pilgrimage. The rough walls were painted white and a contrasting dark concrete forms the roof, which famously curves to one side. Unevenly shaped windows dot one wall of the building. The windows are deep and filled with hand-painted glass. It is a strange building with very thick walls but a small interior space. On the inside the light shines through the asymmetric windows dimly but dynamically. The interior is very plain and modest with unadorned pews only on the south side. The walls, roof, and floor all curve down toward the altar.

Preserving a Landmark

In 2014 the Notre-Dame du Haut chapel was attacked by vandals who broke a hand-painted glass window and stole a concrete collection box. The incident raised questions about the lack of security at the landmark chapel. People also began to speak out about the structure's deterioration due to moisture issues and aging masonry. The incident sparked a fierce discussion about balancing the money made from historical landmark ticket sales versus the amount of money spent to take care of it.

LUDWIG MIES VAN DER ROHE

The International Style

Ludwig Mies van der Rohe (1886–1969) is regarded as one of the foremost pioneers in modern architecture. He was one of the cultural refugees of Nazi Germany who sought safe haven in the United States. Mies had been running the Bauhaus School in Dessau, working to stamp out the heavy politicism that was both distracting and calling too much attention to the school. Despite his best efforts, Hitler would not shake his distrust of the institution and decreed Mies's work "un-German." The United States was thrilled to have him, as well as his contemporaries Walter Gropius, Peter Behrens, and Le Corbusier who quickly became leaders of the Modernist movement.

After World War I, Mies had been searching for a style that could rebuild Europe. He thought a lot about the achievements of the historical styles, especially Gothic and Classical and wanted to find something as powerful but more tailored to modern times. He had received a foundation in practical construction from his father, who had been a stonemason in Germany. He worked as an assistant in the prestigious office of Peter Behrens and as a furniture designer for Bruno Paul (1874–1968).

First Designs

After World War I, Mies became famous for a series of projects he designed that were never actually built. These projects stimulated many new ideas about the shape of structures and materials used to build them. For example, he designed a twenty-story skyscraper with a steel frame that was completely sheathed in glass to make it appear transparent. He expanded on that even further with another design for a thirty-story skyscraper with irregular lines at the perimeter that were intended to catch light and cast reflections. He developed another office block out of concrete, an unusual material selection for the time. Each of the seven floors carried a cantilever, or horizontal windows that ran in a continuous strip. In this example you can see Frank Lloyd Wright's influence. These buildings were strikingly plain, with no exterior ornamentation. The interiors were defined by open floor plans and flexibility in space. These buildings exuded function and rationality.

Mies's Maxims

Mies's proverbial wisdoms about architecture were so powerful that they have since spilled over into all design sensibilities for everything from furniture to fashion.

- "God is in the details."
- "Less is more."

Barcelona Pavilion

One of the most celebrated architectural designs of the twentieth century was Mies's Barcelona Pavilion, which he built for the 1929 International Exposition in Barcelona. It was a relatively small building that did not include any displays. It was only one story but elevated slightly, which made it appear more important than the other buildings that surrounded it. It contained eight simple, unadorned columns made of chromium-painted steel that supported a flat, concrete slab roof. The walls were not aligned or even incorporated with the columns, which made it look as if the roof was floating above the vertical walls. Inside, the floors were made of Roman travertine and the windows were tinted. There was an exterior courtyard that contained a reflecting pool holding the single decoration in the entire exhibit: a sculpture of a dancing girl (by Georg Kolbe). Mies himself designed stainless-steel tables, stools, and chairs for the building. The tufted chairs were covered in white kid upholstery.

The Barcelona Pavilion embodied what we have come to know as Modern design. It was a straightforward expression of architecture without lavish ornamentation. The composition was established by wide plains and simple geometric forms that allowed the quality design materials and craftsmanship to take center spotlight. The original was dismantled soon after the exposition but a replica has since been reconstructed at the site.

Farnsworth House

The Farnsworth House (1946–1951) was the residential answer to the Barcelona Pavilion. The house, built as a weekend getaway in Plano, Illinois, was reduced to the simplest elements: one floor, steel frame, and glass curtain walls. It was raised slightly off the ground, which lent some strength to the elegant form. The interior maximized space with an open floor plan, and a single terrace jutted off to one side. One of the few interruptions to the interior space was a fireplace that was placed at the core of the house. Two wide sets of steps lead from the ground to the porch and then from the porch to the terrace. The house was harmonious with the natural landscape that surrounded it; only the light-colored steel window frames distinguished it from its environment.

The house became a proud example of Modernism and the International style but in truth, it may not have been the most practical structure for domestic living. For one thing, the house was like a very large transparent rectangle and it did not lend itself well to privacy. The glass, which was not protected by screens, offered little protection from the harshest climates, letting in the buggy summer heat and filling with droplets of condensation in the winter.

Seagram Building

The Seagram Building (1954–1958) was highly influential and did much to determine the look and scope of New York architecture from the late 1950s onward. Avant-garde for its time, the thirty-eight-story office building is set on bronze-clad pillars. The façade includes alternating strips of bronze plating and tinted glass. It was the first building designed with floor-to-ceiling windows—the first with a true glass curtain. Vertical bronze I-beams between the windows emphasize the vertical expanse of the building. The building carried no ornamental façades, stone, or brick. The interior design was sleek and minimalist with travertine, marble, and bronze details.

The building was set back a bit from the street, leaving a large open space in front that was intended for pedestrians. This space, which came to be known as an urban plaza, would soon become a common feature in most New York City skyscrapers.

Recognizing the International Style

International style is the most common style of architecture for commercial buildings in the United States today. Here are some of the main features:

- Walls made of thin material like glass or concrete
- High-quality materials, especially on the interior, like marble and bronze
- Rectilinear forms
- Absolute perfection in composition and details
- Little or no ornamentation
- The presence of cantilevers
- Glass and steel façades
- Open interior spaces

DECONSTRUCTION

Chaotic Style

Deconstructivist style is part of the Post-Modern era. It was used most heavily in the late 1980s. During the movement's heyday in the late 1980s, the Museum of Modern Art (MoMA) in New York City hosted an exhibit called Deconstructivist Architecture. The exhibit, though, was more of an introduction and exploration of the style because it was still emerging. The MoMA recognized seven architects who were at the helm of this style: Frank Gehry, Zaha Hadid, Rem Koolhaas, Wolf D. Prix, Daniel Libeskind, Bernard Tschumi, and Peter Eisenman.

Deconstructivist architecture involves twisting, curving forms that seem to almost fragment and dislodge the framework or skeleton of a building. The resulting aesthetic is chaotic and unpredictable and sometimes leaves observers feeling unhinged or disturbed. Practitioners of Deconstructivist architecture find Modernism to be too constraining with rules that place too many limitations on the possibilities of form. These architects are not overly concerned with ornament as a fixture because they believe that if something has been thoughtfully designed, the resulting look is ornamentation enough. The geometry that appears in Deconstructivist buildings often echoes abstract expressionism and cubist art.

Russian Constructivism as Inspiration

Russian Constructivism was developed by the Russian avant-garde in the early twentieth century. It was technically an offshoot of

Modernism but the resulting look was very abstract and experimental. Constructivists pared down art to its most basic elements, and kept things minimal when piecing them back together into something orderly. The Model of the Monument to the Third International (1919), for example, designed by Vladimir Tatlin (1885–1953) was the proposal for a double-spiral tower that would house office buildings. However, the 1,300-foot structure was never built.

The tower would have involved new materials and technological building methods to construct an iron frame that would cover a glass cylinder, cube, and cone. Tatlin cast off the idea of walls and instead asserted an open frame. A lot of the plans for Russian Constructivist buildings were never realized because they were not possible. Postwar Russia did not have the resources or innovations necessary to build them. However, pictures of models like Tatlin's monument made their way around the world and their bold, fantastic style made a strong impact.

Futurism

Futurism, like Constructivism, was a postwar movement that started in Italy. Futurists were trying to inject life into Italian architecture, which they found to be worn out. They preferred plain and honest designs where even the most unglamorous elements—like elevator shafts—remained in the open, not hidden from view.

Peter Eisenman

Peter Eisenman was born in 1932 in Newark, New Jersey. He studied at Cornell University and one of his earliest jobs was working for Walter Gropius. He is an architectural theorist who has drawn ideas from Nietzsche and Noam Chomsky. To him, Post-Modernism should intertwine philosophy and linguistics. These theories had a major impact on the architectural discipline and are evident in everything he has built.

Eisenman first gained attention for a series of houses, which were simply assigned a number one through ten, designed in the late sixties and early seventies. Most of these homes were just ideas that had been worked into formal plans but never actually built. Some of these houses disoriented people because of details like nonengaged columns and stairways that led to nowhere. He constantly rejected the principles of Modernism and the functional sensibilities that accompanied them. Some observers called his numbered houses "nihilistic." Eisenman was particularly interested with taking the traditional elements of a building and rotating them from where they might be typically positioned. This made them appear to be a framework, and moving them around so that the structure looked a bit confused and disoriented. These manipulations formed interesting spaces on the inside of the buildings. Later, he designed the Berlin Museum as part of the International Building Exhibition in Berlin in 1987.

Eisenman and Chomsky

Eisenman believed that the meaning of a structure was more important than its form. His designs were not very clear or rational at first look. But he was taken with famous linguist Noam Chomsky's work on expression. He believed that since we all come from the same linguistic background and therefore learn to express ourselves similarly, we should all be able to look at his architecture and understand his meaning. In that way, he believed his buildings conveyed a narrative component.

Memorial to the Murdered Jews of Europe

The Memorial to the Murdered Jews of Europe (2005) is located between the former East and West Berlin. Eisenman believed that anything involving the memory of the Holocaust needed to be somber. While most memorials are celebrations of life, this memorial needed to honor the victims and never forget the tragedy of mass death. The resulting plan was abstract. He positioned more than 2,700 large rectangular steles of varying sizes and shapes on a sloped piece of land. There are no words or engravings, no plaques, no inscriptions on the stone slabs. There is an air of anonymity. Visitors move through the memorial by maneuvering through disorienting passageways between the stones. The spaces between them narrow and widen while the ground slopes at different angles. Eisenman likened this experience to what Jews went through socially and physically during the Holocaust.

Eisenman's design for the monument stirred up a lot of controversy when he first presented it. People were put off by the abstract design and harsh symbolism. They thought that a war memorial should be more informational. Eventually, to calm some of these complaints, the monument added a visitors' center at the entrance with historical information and artifacts on view.

Preventing Vandalism

There was some concern about vandalism at the Memorial to the Murdered Jews of Europe when it was first built. Nothing would be more horrible than someone desecrating a monument to such a sensitive cause. The slabs are coated with a special solution that prevents any graffiti from sticking to them.

FRANK GEHRY

A Neo-Modernist

Frank Gehry was born in Canada in 1929 and moved to California with his parents when he was in his late teens. He proved to be creative at a young age, building imaginary homes and cities from items he found at his grandfather's hardware store. He attended the University of Southern California for undergraduate school and was then accepted into Harvard's architecture school. He dropped out to return to Los Angeles where he began a cardboard furniture line in the 1970s called Easy Edges.

These cardboard furniture pieces were Gehry's first attempt at designing something that was functional and yet visually striking. The earliest pieces were made with corrugated cardboard, layered so that they were durable enough for people to sit on or use for tables. The furniture was very elegant, such as the "wiggle chair," which was a straight-backed chair that faded into three curving ripples. These ripples buoyed the chair from the ground. To make them this strong, he manipulated sixty layers of cardboard and held them together with hidden screws. Finally, he edged the piece in wood. He created a second line of furniture called Experimental Edges that was rougher in appearance with bulkier pieces of imperfectly stacked cardboard and unfinished edges.

His designs were a reaction to the Modernist forms that to him seemed cold and sterile.

Danziger House

Gehry established his architecture practice in Los Angeles in the early 1960s. In 1965 Gehry designed the Danziger House, a studio for designer Louis Danziger. The structure looked like a plain box made of concrete. It reflected Gehry's admiration of Louis Kahn, a champion of functionalism. He used simple materials, like concrete, and arranged them in a way to maximize daylight. The unique structure brought Gehry attention as a principal architect.

Gehry House

Gehry's early works showed a reverence for the undone. His house in Santa Monica, California (Gehry House, 1977–1978), could easily be confused with a construction site. He essentially took off the outer layers of the original Dutch Colonial Revival house right down to the beams. Then he wrapped a new house around it. To unnerved neighbors, it was a garish mess of plywood, ribbed metal siding, glass, and chain-link fencing. To a growing base of admirers, however, it was a sculpture . . . in which you could live. The house became an outstanding example of Deconstructivist style.

Soon Gehry was earning a number of commissions for residential properties around Los Angeles. Critics believed that his designs did not make the best use of urban space or the contexts in which they were to be built. That said, one couldn't deny how capable he was at negotiating the chaotic environment, tight lots, and small budgets. His work urged people to think about the possibilities of architecture as art even in ordinary circumstances. Gehry took on a variety of commissions: public buildings, concert halls, restaurants, and museums. His body of work grew so large that he was honored with the prestigious Pritzker Prize, an honor set aside for those who have made the greatest contributions to the field of architecture.

Pritzker Architecture Prize

The prize is sponsored by the Pritzkers, a Chicago-based family who own the Hyatt hotel chain. Each spring, the winner is awarded $100,000 and a bronze medallion based on Louis Henry Sullivan's designs.

Guggenheim Museum Bilbao

Bilbao had previously been a hub for the ETA (Euskadi ta Askatasuna, or the Basque Homeland and Liberty), a radical separatist organization that led the Basque National Liberation Movement. Viewed as terrorists by many, the ETA was credited with a number of murders and kidnappings, car bombs, violent acts against public transportation and public buildings, graffiti, and riots. The port fell into disrepair and was no longer a bustling source of income. Amid the violence and changing economy, Bilbao fell into an economic and cultural slump.

Leaders began a focused urban renewal campaign in the 1990s. The Guggenheim Museum (1997) was the first in a line of major investments in the region. The government pitched the idea to the Solomon R. Guggenheim Foundation, agreeing to fund the project and to donate the Bilbao port area as a location. The foundation, in the meantime, commissioned Frank Gehry to design the building that would ultimately become the most recognized symbol of Bilbao's rebirth. The museum was built to look like a giant ship in reverence of Bilbao's history as a powerful port. Extraordinary curves made from a steel frame seem to twist, each stacked on top of each other, covered with luminous titanium tiles that capture the sunlight. The central atrium towers, with dynamic space, stone, light, and metal, bend their way to the top to the point of exhilaration. The atrium connects to whimsical galleries that boast their own unique shapes: a trapezoid, L-shaped, and a long narrow galley.

Disney Concert Hall

In 1988 Gehry was commissioned to design the Walt Disney Concert Hall in downtown Los Angeles. His appreciation for unusual shapes and confusing stacks was opportune for a traditional concert hall in which function dictates that a number of rooms of various sizes without windows must all be focused on a single stage. Since the concert hall was home to the Los Angeles Philharmonic, considerations about things such as acoustics and positioning of the concert organ were crucial. The remarkable building—about which critics have said that the sound is terrific—has a Douglas-fir ceiling and hall, and oak floors.

Features of Gehry Designs
- Free-form construction of shapes
- Sculptural quality
- Curling and flowing shapes
- Drawing connections between the building and the site

ALDO ROSSI

Working in the Context of the City

Born in Milan, Italy, to a bicycle manufacturer, Aldo Rossi (1931–1997) received an architecture degree in 1959 from the Polytechnic University of Milan. He served as editor of an architectural magazine called *Casabella* from 1955 to 1964. He was known internationally not just for his architecture but also his big drawings and influential theories. His work was intensely focused on emphasizing his social perspective. Rossi wrote, designed furniture, and painted. In the 1960s he began teaching, which he did for the rest of his life.

Rossi's *The Architecture of the City*

Rossi wrote a powerful book called *The Architecture of the City* in 1966. In it, he presented the story of architecture and urban theory. He argued against the Modern movement and the functionalism that accompanies it. As a Post-Modernist, he pushed for a reclaiming of classicism and a renewed emphasis on craft. He was preoccupied with the topic of city neglect and believed that architects should build structures that work within the context of their cities instead of trying to shock and awe with something brazenly modern. This perspective became known as Nonrationalist.

Cemetery of San Cataldo

The San Cataldo Cemetery (1971–1984) in Modena was an extension of a cemetery at the same site that Cesare Costa designed in the nineteenth century. Rossi submitted his plan to a competition and won the commission. Just before beginning work on the design and construction of the cemetery, Rossi survived a car accident and was hospitalized. He had a lot of time to think while he was recovering. He had written about "fragments" in architecture and now he envisioned his broken body as a series of pieces that needed to be reassembled in order to mend. This vision is apparent in his final design at the cemetery.

The area is enclosed with a wall. A desolate structure near the entrance gate looks like an abandoned building but is actually a temple. This lonely structure is a nondenominational venue for funeral services. A smokestack is a symbol of a communal grave for the unknown dead. As you walk through the site, you must pass through successive rectangles that get taller and thinner as they progress.

Rossi's design is so free of ornamentation that some people find it to be disturbing because of the severity of the open spaces where there should be a roof and doors. Some of the openings let in light and others hold cremated bodies. In his book, *A Scientific Autobiography*, Rossi distinguishes between cities for the living and cemeteries as cities for the dead. The fact that the interior has no roof is intended to symbolize the fact that when you are dead, you will not need a roof or shelter. Walking through the cemetery is like a metaphysical experience because it forces visitors to walk through death.

A Floating Theater

In 1979 Rossi designed a floating theater to commemorate the Venice Biennale, a contemporary art exhibit that occurs every other year. It was towed out to the Punta della Dogana, an art museum on the Grand Canal in Venice. The theater seated 250 around one central stage with an octagonal-shaped tower. It echoed the Venetian floating theaters of the past.

Rebuilding Berlin

Rossi was very active in a large campaign to revitalize Berlin in the 1980s. Berlin had been through a lot throughout the twentieth century and its infrastructure had suffered.

Berlin's Troubled Past

Berlin had experienced strife throughout the twentieth century:

- 1920s: Economic devastation
- 1930s: Nazi takeover
- 1940s: Allied bombing raids
- 1960s–1980s: The Berlin wall

Despite its complicated history, Berlin was still revered as the birthplace of Modernism. In the eighties Berlin launched a new campaign to rebuild and reinvigorate with special attention to restoring its architectural roots. In the late 1970s West Germany established the International Building Exhibition to clean up and develop the dead zones and eyesores around the city. They wanted to turn these areas into buildings and apartments. A couple hundred architects from all over the world threw their hats into the competitions for commissions. Aldo Rossi was one of them. He was ultimately involved in designing a number of buildings during the campaign in the mid-1980s.

One of the goals of the campaign to restore Berlin was to honor the traditions of the buildings already developed in the area. For example, structures in Berlin were limited to a six-story height. Also, houses came right up to the sidewalk and included courtyards and large hallways for the public. The city was also lively. To preserve the city's diversity, one architect was assigned a block for which he would create a master plan. Then a group of architects would each be given a building on the block to complete in their own way.

One of Rossi's most popular buildings was an understated structure made of red brick and yellow blocks. He used colored bands and I-beam lintels over the windows to show how the building had been constructed. After the fall of the wall in 1989, Rossi redesigned the Quartier Schützenstrasse, which had previously been a border strip associated with Allied Checkpoint Charlie. This area, still considered a major world interest in the Cold War, was a disaster at the time the wall came down.

Rossi in his typical style developed buildings that recalled the historic cityscape. He divided the site into smaller plots using multicolored façades and roofs. He included a replica of Michelangelo's courtyard façade at Rome's Palazzo Farnese (an important building in the Renaissance).

The total number of façades is actually more than the number of houses. Most buildings are residential; the rest are a mix of commercial and residential. Two large and two small interior courtyards bring light to the block. The colors are supposed to recall colors of antique architecture: bright red and green aluminum, muted red, blue, and yellow for stucco. The stone was light gray and pink. The design included exposed sheet metal. Windows vary in shape and there are attics. He wanted it to look like a city within a city.

BRIDGES

Spanning the Distance

Bridges are amazing pieces of architecture. Many are beautifully designed, and often they become iconic symbols of the city in which they are situated, as is the case with London's Tower Bridge or New York's Brooklyn Bridge. Aside from their stunning appearance, what is remarkable is that they show everything about how they are built. Supports and framework are not hidden behind walls or façades. Their design tells us everything about how they work.

Five basic bridges are:

1. Suspension
2. Cable
3. Truss
4. Arch
5. Beam

Golden Gate Bridge

In the 1930s, the Golden Gate Bridge was built to connect northern California to Marin County. Until then, the only way to get across the San Francisco Bay was by ferry. As the region became more populated there were more people trying to cross the water and there were not nearly enough ferries to accommodate them. People were also beginning to own their own cars and wanted to drive themselves instead of depending on public transportation. Several plans were discussed for connecting the two sides of the bay—at one time city officials even considered including railroad ties for train access. After some deliberation, state officials decided to construct a bridge for automobiles and the project was made possible in part thanks to the Hoover Administration which, at the time, was pushing for bridge building across the country as a way to create jobs. Architect and engineer Joseph Strauss began to plan the longest bridge that had ever been built. The bay was deep and weather conditions were often treacherous due to high winds and strong water currents. Although he had already designed hundreds of bridges, this would prove to be the most difficult project of his career.

In suspension bridge construction, the cables are stretched over the towers, so that they pull the entire structure down and straight on both sides. Since this is such a long bridge, running the cables continuously over the tops of the two identical towers keeps them from bending. The cables are then stretched to land on either side of the bridge and held in place by concrete anchorages.

The two identical towers are planted deep into the bay floor on either side and stabilized by crossbars that help them to stay firm in the bay winds.

Building the cables was an enormous task. The cables were so big that they needed to be built onsite because there was not a vehicle big enough to transport them had they been prefabricated elsewhere. There are two main cables that pass over the tops of the towers and run to the anchorages on the shore. Each cable was fashioned from sixty-one separate strands that were each spun from a long, continuous piece of wire. The resultant cables are more than three feet in diameter, incredibly solid and strong. About every fifty feet on the cable is a band that clamps a suspender rope. The roadway is supported in part by the trusses that run underneath it, but these trusses are held up by suspender ropes. These suspender ropes are about two feet in diameter and were permanently fused into sockets with molten liquid zinc. Workers had to build both sides very carefully to make sure that the whole structure did not buckle.

Cable-Stayed Bridges

Cable bridges look a lot like suspension bridges but in reality are quite different. Remember, on a suspension bridge, the two largest cables run over the towers to anchorages on the shore. The road is attached to the suspension cables that hang from these main cables. On a cable bridge, cables are actually attached to the towers that carry the load. These cables can be attached to the towers by several different methods. In a radial system, cables extend from several different points on the road to a single point on top of the tower. In a parallel configuration, the points run along the height of the tower and the cables run parallel from them. Today, cable-stayed bridges are growing in popularity in the United States because they require much less building materials and are therefore less expensive and faster to construct. A cable-stayed is planned for the New Tappan Zee in New York. The Arthur Ravenel Jr. Bridge in Charleston, SC (2005) is an example of a radial cable-stayed bridge.

Truss Bridge

A truss bridge is made from a series of steel bars. These bars are then fashioned into triangles, almost like latticework. The forces are concentrated into this network of triangles, which in turn provide enough support for the heavy loads that cross the bridge. The truss bends a little under the weight of the traffic that crosses it. This bending causes compression in the top horizontal beams and tension in the bottom horizontal beams. Then each of the vertical and diagonal beams experience either tension or compression depending on their direction. Trusses are often used in conjunction with other building methods as we saw with the Golden Gate Bridge. The New River Gorge Bridge in Fayetteville, West Virginia (1977) is a steel construction that combines truss and arch design.

Cantilevered bridges can be simple, such as a beam that forms a footbridge. Most modern cantilevered bridges, however, are complex versions of the truss. Supports are positioned at either end from which strong, straight steel arms extend. Diagonal steel tubes come from the top and the bottom of each support to hold the arms in place. From these arms, platforms project horizontally to span a space. The Forth Rail Bridge in Scotland (1890) is an example of this type of bridge.

Roman Trusses

The Romans, who were major innovators in bridge design, used trusses. Trajan's Column in Rome illustrates the epic wars between the Romans and Dacians through a huge relief that spirals up the height of the column. The images celebrate Trajan's victory over the Dacians. Included in the over 150 scenes is a depiction of Apollodorus's trussed bridge across the Danube.

Arch

In an arch bridge, the curved design provides the support needed to bear heavy loads. The weight of the traffic on the roadway creates compression forces. The curved design of the supports under the roadway then sends these forces down around the lines of the curve instead of straight down. The foundation supports absorb theses forces and hold the bridge in a strong, stationary position. The Romans built more than a thousand arch bridges, mostly circular arches, and they were so strong and stable that many of them are still standing today, like the Pont du Gard that we discussed earlier over the Gard River in what is today southern France.

Beam

The beam is the most common bridge type and can be as simple as a single beam stretching over an expanse between two supports. The beam bends, allowing the structure to carry the traffic above it. As it bends, the top experiences horizontal compression and the bottom experiences horizontal tension. Then, the weight of the load on the beam is sent straight down onto the supports. The closer together the supports are, the stronger the beam bridge. For this reason, beam bridges do not span very long distances. "Continuous span bridges" are a number of beam bridges together in a chain to make one long bridge.

The Longest Bridge

The Lake Pontchartrain Causeway in Louisiana is a twenty-four-mile-long continuous span bridge. It is so long that for eight of those miles you cannot see land in any direction. It is listed in *Guinness World Records* as the longest continuous bridge that passes over water. It involves 2,243 separate spans for the southbound lane. There are 1,500 spans on the northbound lane.

MID-CENTURY MODERN

America's Housing Boom

After World War II, the United States experienced an economic boom. Middle-class Americans were wealthy in a way that was unknown before the war. Congress passed the GI Bill in 1944, which gave veterans money to go to college and purchase homes. There had been a housing shortage in the Depression and during the war years but now mortgages were affordable and easy to obtain. A housing boom ensued. New technologies made it possible to prefabricate houses and other building structures. During this period a new version of the International style emerged that we refer to as Mid-Century Modern.

The style manifested itself in homes built from 1945 to the 1980s. They tended to be built on long, flat planes. Often they boasted very large windows that spotlighted nature and an open floor plan.

Common Features of Mid-Century Modern Homes
- Flat roofs
- Ranches with gabled roofs
- Large windows
- Sliding glass doors
- Interior spaces distinguished by steps so as to create a slight elevation
- Outdoor access in multiple rooms
- Views of the landscape from all rooms

Case Study House Program

The Case Study House Program started in Los Angeles in 1945 as a postwar residential experiment. The idea was to expose middle-class Americans to Modernism through residential architecture. John Entenza, an editor at *Arts & Architecture*, a progressive magazine, wrote about the ways to offer cost-efficient housing to the public. He got manufacturers to donate materials and organized architects who could build these low-cost homes with a modern design for clients. He then used the magazine to publicize the initiative and everyone's role in it.

The architects he invited to join his group included Charles and Ray Eames, Richard Neutra, Eero Saarinen, and Pierre Koenig. Not all of the plans developed were actually built, and frequently a house plan would change dramatically between design phase and construction. Many times these changes happened when certain building materials were not available. Those that were built provided fantastic Mid-Century residential architecture that would influence American architectural trends in years to come. These homes made Los Angeles the hub of American Mid-Century Modernism. Today, ten of the Los Angeles Case Study Houses have been added to the National Register of Historic Places.

Case Study House #22

Number 22 was the most iconic Case Study House. It was designed by Pierre Koenig as a primarily glass structure perched high in the Hollywood Hills, overlooking Los Angeles. The owner, Buck Stahl, wanted to build a glass and steel house for his family. He started the work but Koenig took over after a few years. It was a 2,200-square-foot home with two bedrooms. The house was built to embrace what was considered to be the modern lifestyle.

Koenig carefully situated the private and communal areas of the house apart from each other. A hallway connects the two wings but the two sections of the house remain spatially separated. Walking through the house, residents and visitors experience the panoramic views afforded by the lot. The living area of the home holds the only solid wall—which is backed against the carport and the street.

Richard Neutra

Richard Neutra (1892–1970) was one of the United States' most significant modern architects in the Mid-Century era. He studied under Adolf Loos at Vienna University of Technology and later took a job working for Erich Mendelsohn. He also spent time working under Frank Lloyd Wright. His designs allowed for a great deal of natural light, and the houses were often prefabricated. He was able to personalize a space to suit the homeowner's taste and the landscape in a way that had not been done before.

Julius Shulman

The Case Study Houses were immortalized by famous architectural photographer Julius Shulman (1910–2009). Shulman established the identity of Mid-Century Modern and then spread it through mass-market magazines such as *Good Housekeeping* and *House & Garden* so that all Americans could see it. He photographed dozens of homes from most of the top Modern architects of the twentieth century, building their reputations and putting a spotlight on the discipline. He was especially close to the California architectural scene and helped to develop an image of the California modern lifestyle and casual living. The photos depict light-filled homes made of glass with crystal pools and gorgeous landscapes. He photographed buildings by Ray and Charles Eames, and Oscar Niemeyer. His images heavily influenced the way modern architecture was understood and taught.

He was born in Brooklyn in 1910 and moved to a Connecticut farm, which ignited his love of nature. When he was ten he moved with his family to Los Angeles. The first Modern house he ever saw was one of Neutra's designs. He was so intrigued that he began to photograph it. Then he gave his photograph to Neutra's draftsman who then passed them on to Neutra. When Neutra saw the pictures, he loved them and invited Shulman to come photograph more projects. Neutra mentored him in the principles and forms of architecture and introduced him to other architects. Soon, he was a fixture in the Modern movement.

Charles and Ray Eames

This husband and wife team were involved in the Case Study Houses. They also became famous for their furniture designs, which are still coveted today. Their chairs experimented with all kinds of materials: wire mesh, fiberglass, resin. The Eames Lounge Chair, designed for the Herman Miller Furniture Company, is the most iconic of their pieces. This was a chair and ottoman set made of molded plywood with leather seats.

NORMAN FOSTER

A High-Tech Architect

Norman Foster (1935–) is heralded as a Modernist who embraces both technology and green architecture. He emphasizes the importance of quality materials with as much dedication as the Arts and Crafts architects before him. He believes that environmentalism is fashionable and that, if executed properly in the spaces we build, green architecture should celebrate the way we live. He was trained at the University of Manchester in England before attending Yale in New Haven, Connecticut. His buildings are typically sleek and made with mostly steel and glass.

Sheds

Foster explored the technological possibilities of developing structures that were surrounded by lightweight shells called sheds. These sheds function like the exoskeleton on an insect.

High-Tech Architecture

Foster's work has been referred to as High-Tech architecture, sometimes also known as Late Modernism or Structural Expressionism, a style that emerged in the late 1970s. Buildings in this subdiscipline are high-functioning structures that incorporate technology and run almost like machines. They are built with industrial materials like steel, aluminum, and glass and often incorporate bright-colored beams and girders. The structures that support these high-tech buildings, like elevator shafts and ductwork, are often placed on the exterior instead of tucked away in an inconspicuous area of the interior. Placing these elements on the outside heavily impacts the aesthetic of the exterior of the building but it also leaves the interiors wide open and flexible for design and function.

Second Chicago School

The Second Chicago School was inspired by the modernist movement from the Berlin architects who moved to the United States during World War II, such as Ludwig Mies van der Rohe who came to Chicago to be the dean in the architecture department at what is now the Illinois Institute of Technology.

Willis Faber and Dumas Headquarters

Foster and his partners designed the Willis Faber and Dumas Headquarters (1971–1975) in Ipswich, England, almost as a revolt against the traditional office building format of isolated offices and reception areas that were accessible by elevators. It is a three-story building with a wide-open plan and an escalator connecting floors that would typically be considered very walkable. The building houses 1,300 office staff. The architects were already anticipating how the Information Age would stretch the facilities in office buildings so they raised the office floors, which left room for computer wires and connection boards. These floors are cantilevered concrete slabs that are supported by a grid of concrete pillars.

Foster included decidedly non-work-related features such as a swimming pool, a rooftop garden, and a restaurant, which brought an unusual social component to the workplace (the pool has since been covered up to accommodate more office space. Since this is a registered building, they were unable to fill the pool completely and instead they placed a false floor so that the old pool is still visible). The city is an old medieval town and the exterior was planned so that it would fit in to the old setting. For example, the façade is curved so that it aligns with the irregular medieval street line. The curtain wall is sheathed in square glass panels that are tinted and glazed and fitted into place with silicon joints. The glass curtain wall is suspended from the roof with a clamping strip and braced the entire way down by internal glass pieces that are not visible from the exterior. These glass pieces form a bracing system that keeps the building rigid in the wind.

The building also pioneered low energy consumption. The roof is heavily insulated with a thick layer of dirt and grass, which promotes good thermal performance on the interior.

In 1991, the Willis Building (as it is now known) was given a Grade I listing, a British honor, which means that the building can never be altered or demolished without obtaining special permission from the government. This is the youngest building to ever achieve that distinction; usually a building must be over thirty years old to be considered. Listed buildings are placed on the Statutory List of Buildings of Special Architectural or Historic Interest. Generally all structures that were built pre-1870 are listed. There are nearly 500,000 buildings included on the list. Only 2.5 percent of all buildings in the UK are considered Grade I. These buildings are so important that they are often recognized internationally. Ancient sites that are no longer inhabited, like Stonehenge, are listed separately as Scheduled Ancient Monuments.

Hongkong and Shanghai Banking Corporation Headquarters

One of Foster and Partners' first buildings to garner major international attention was the Hongkong and Shanghai Banking

Corporation (HSBC) Headquarters (1979–1986). It is a stepped rectangle sheathed in glass with a steel exoskeleton. The resulting aesthetic is very futuristic. The elevators are placed on the outside of the building, leaving open interior spaces and also making it easy to service the elevators. The building boasts extraordinary views of both Victoria Harbor and Victoria Peak.

Eight exterior steel trusses form the floors. These trusses divide the building into zones or modules, five in total. The zones each have their own network of escalators. At the level of each horizontal truss is a floor with double-height ceilings that holds conference rooms, food and recreation areas, and external terraces.

Public banking areas are positioned on the third–twelfth floors in a center atrium. With energy conservation in mind, this section is lit by mirrors outside the building that adjust to follow the sun's path. At the ground level is a huge open plaza. Escalators carry visitors up through a glass ceiling to the atrium.

Beijing Capital International Airport Terminal 3

Beijing Airport Terminal 3 (2003–2008) has been called one of the best airports because it is simple and bright—attributes that are not always apparent in airport architecture. At the time it was built it was the first building to surpass the million-square-meter mark. The structure needs to be huge because it houses 126 aircraft stands. High glass walls form a vault on the interior. Domestic travel gates are at two sides of the front triangle. This keeps people from having to walk too far to another concourse.

The plan is wide at the arrival end so that passengers from both international and domestic flights are processed in the same place. The space is long and narrow which makes it straightforward to navigate but also maximizes the light.

Exterior details include red columns and a curved overhanging roof. The plan makes it perfectly clear where you need to go whether you are headed to pick up your bags or have your visa processed. Foster was especially thinking of the latter. He wanted to greet international passengers with an experience as they get off the planes, instead of corralling them down dingy corridors. A high-speed people mover shuttles passengers to their gates. Skylights face the southeast to get the best from the early morning sun, which adds light and warmth, therefore minimizing the need for manufactured energy.

GREEN ARCHITECTURE
Responsible Building

Green architecture or, as it is sometimes called, sustainable architecture, aims to minimize the impact of building on the environment. Practitioners of green architecture consider the impact of materials on human health. They emphasize the importance of using local, nonsynthetic products, harvesting natural resources responsibly, recycling, and reusing materials from previous structures. Green architecture also stresses the importance of space efficiency. Developing structures and communities that will not strain natural resources or the environment ensures availability for future generations. This means considering the renewable resources like water and energy sources such as solar.

California Academy of Sciences

Renzo Piano (1937–) designed a green roof for the California Academy of Sciences (2005–2008) that completely embodies these green building principles. The roof of the building was made of rolling terrain, and more than 1.7 million plants from nine different native species were planted on top of it. This provided a habitat for wildlife and encouraged settling of some endangered species such as the San Bruno butterfly. One of the earthen mounds forms a dome over a manufactured rainforest that stands four stories high. Mechanical windows were installed so that light and air can enter. A planetarium sits under the second mound. Right in the middle is an open-air piazza. Most of the administrative offices are situated so that they can receive natural light. The mound construction of the roof allows cool air to circulate down into the interior spaces underneath it. It also works to collect rainwater.

The roof soil provides an additional six inches of insulation. Below, the floors are heated by radiant hot water. There are also skylights for ventilation, heating, and air conditioning. The builders used steel from recycled sources. They harvested timber from yield forests. They recycled almost all the demolition debris and donated 32,000 tons of sand to local initiatives that were funding projects to restore dunes.

LEED Certification

The U.S. Green Building Council (USGBC) runs a program called LEED (Leadership in Energy and Environmental Design), a green building certificate program. LEED certification is an honor and they search for the most high-performing green buildings. They rate projects that fall into the following categories:

- Building design and construction
- Interior design and construction
- Building operations and maintenance
- Neighborhood development
- Homes

LEED is an internationally recognized ranking system that uses a combination of credit categories like location and transportation, energy and atmosphere, water efficiency, and indoor environmental quality. Based on these categories, a project can earn points. The number of points determines the level of LEED certification. The levels are certified silver, gold or, best of all, platinum.

Phipps Conservatory

The Phipps Conservatory and Botanical Gardens in Pittsburgh, Pennsylvania, developed the Center for Sustainable Landscapes. It has received all the highest certifications including the Living Building Challenge, LEED platinum (one of the highest points ever awarded). It was built over a site that was previously a brownfield that had been paved over. Onsite solar photovoltaics meet 99 percent of the structure's energy needs. A single wind turbine meets the rest. There are also fourteen geothermal wells. The structure uses half the energy of a comparable office building.

The building achieves net-zero water by treating all gray water and black water onsite. It can then be used again for toilet flushing and for irrigating orchids. It also has systems for capturing energy that make sure none goes to waste. They recycle wastewater and collect rainwater, which ensures that the building's owners never have to tap into city water. The area was formerly a brownfield, which means that the land was considered unsafe because of a pollutant.

It has now been completely rehabilitated so that 150 noninvasive local plant species can survive there. The green roof holds eight-inch soil depth, which helps control the temperature in the building and prevents runoff. Wastewater is filtered in the wetland that has been constructed.

Whole-House Systems Approach

This approach considers all parts of a house and how the materials within a house might contribute to the house's efficiency:

- Insulation
- Appliances
- Water heating
- Heating and cooling
- Windows and doors
- Ultra-efficient (renewable energy systems)
- Solar water heating
- Solar electricity

Advanced house framing, also called optimum value engineering, contributes to energy efficiency but also reduces both the amount of lumber used and the amount of waste created.

Some advanced ideas for building include straw bale homes, which involves post-and-beam construction or non-load–bearing construction. Straw bales are then used to fill in the framework. This is a very difficult process. Log homes use logs to provide both walls and insulation. Earth-sheltered homes can be either above or below the ground. These houses allow for ventilation and natural light. This helps with heating and cooling efforts.

Sustainability Treehouse

The Boy Scouts of America established the Sustainability Treehouse (2013) in Glen Jean, West Virginia, as an educational structure. The development coincided with the Boy Scout's new merit badge for sustainability. The architectural firm Mithun funded a sustainable education center. As you learn, you move up through the levels of the forest.

This structure is located in the forest of the Summit Bechtel Reserve. It was designed by Mithun and another firm, BNIM, to have the least possible impact on the environment. The house was built partially from a prefabricated structure; had they prefabricated the entire structure, they would have needed to use cranes that would have done considerable damage to the immediate environment. They used local materials such as black locust wood. Energy is derived from solar panels and two wind turbines and a large cistern that collects and cleanses rainwater. The structure is made of indoor and outdoor platforms that shoot straight up through the forest. Each platform houses an exhibit that allows visitors to learn about the ecosystem. Energy input and output combine to create a structure that yields net-zero energy and net-zero water use. Staircases connect the platforms and stretch from the ground to 125 feet high, above the treetops. Exhibit areas include topics like how to conserve water and tips for energy alternatives.

INDEX